McGRAW-HILL
Language Arts

Vocabulary and Thesaurus
Workbook

Grade 4

McGraw-Hill School Division

New York • Farmington

McGraw-Hill School Division 🜨

A Division of The McGraw·Hill Companies

Copyright McGraw-Hill School Division, a Division of the Educational and Professional Publishing Group of The McGraw-Hill Companies, Inc.

All rights reserved. Permission granted to reproduce for use with McGRAW-HILL LANGUAGE ARTS. No other use of this material or parts thereof, including reproduction, distribution, or storage in an electronic database, permitted without prior written permission of the publisher, except as provided under the United States Copyright Act of 1976.

McGraw-Hill School Division
Two Penn Plaza
New York, New York 10121

Printed in the United States of America

ISBN 0-02-244784-9/4

2 3 4 5 6 7 8 9 009 05 04 03 02 01

TABLE OF CONTENTS

© McGraw-Hill School Division

© McGraw-Hill School Division

Vocabulary: Time-Order Words

Time-order words tell when things happen and the order things happen. Here are some time-order words.

first	next	last week
after	during	before
while	as soon as	later
today	early	then

A. Find the time-order words in the sentences. Write them on the lines.

1. Last week I saw a wren in my backyard.

_____

2. Wrens return early in the spring.

_____

3. They look for nesting places as soon as they arrive.

_____

4. After the pair build a nest, the female lays five to eight eggs.

_____

5. Two weeks later, the baby wrens hatch.

_____

© McGraw-Hill School Division

B. Write the time-order word or phrase that best completes each sentence.

Use capital letters where needed.

| later | as soon as | when | first | during |

6. Some northern birds fly south _____fall arrives.

7. Robins and orioles stay where it is warm _____

the winter.

8. _____the days grow long again, I watch for the birds.

9. The red-wing blackbird is one of the_____

birds I see.

10. The warblers and orioles usually show up much _____ .

C. Complete the paragraph. Write the best word on each line.

| soon | finally | then | first | as soon as |

11.-15. Krista trained the chickadees to eat from her hand._____ she
put up a feeder with seeds in it._____ the birds visited it regularly.
_____ Krista stood near the feeder until the birds got used to her.
Each day she moved a little closer. _____she put the seeds in her
outstretched hand instead of in the feeder. _____ her patience was
rewarded. The chickadees took seeds from her hand!

Writing Activity

Write a paragraph telling about something you did recently.
Place the details in the order in which they happened using
time-order words.

© McGraw-Hill School Division

Idioms

> Sometimes the meaning of a phrase is different from the meanings of the individual words in the phrase. This kind of phrase is called an **idiom**.
>
> The meanings of idioms are in a dictionary. Look up the most important word in the phrase to find the definition of the idiom.

Look at the following idioms which use the word *time*.

*We go there **from time to time.***	sometimes; periodically
*He did it **in no time.***	quickly; very soon
*Joe arrived **on time.***	at the correct time
*See how **time flies!***	time passes quickly
*I had the **time of my life.***	a wonderful time

A. Write the idiom from above that answers each question.

1. What would you say if you had the best time you ever had?

_____

2. Which idiom means "occasionally," or "periodically?"

_____

3. Which idiom can be used instead of this sentence: I can't believe it's

so late! _____

4. Which expression means "something that was done very quickly"?

_____

5. Which idiom would you use if someone arrived exactly when expected?

_____

Go on

© McGraw-Hill School Division

B. Read each question. The idiom is in **bold** type. Look up the underlined word in a dictionary. Use the definition to help you explain your answer to the question.

6. How does something **catch your <u>eye</u>**?

_____

7. If you are **left <u>high</u> and dry**, does it mean you need water?

_____

8. How do you **keep an <u>eye</u> on** something?

_____

9. If you **<u>run</u> out of** milk, does that mean you were in the milk?

_____

10. "If I **<u>take</u> after** my Mom," said Sandy. "Does that mean I follow behind her?"

_____

11. If a car **<u>pulls</u> up** to a store, is it lifting the store into the air?

_____

12. If someone **<u>drives</u> you crazy**, does it mean they have a car or a bus?

_____

13. If you **<u>sign</u> up** for something, are you holding a sign?

_____

14. If you see a little child **<u>act</u> up**, are you watching a play?

_____

15. If you have to **<u>let</u> out** your belt, were you keeping your belt in a cage?

_____

Writing Activity

Think of four idioms and write them down. Then write a funny paragraph using the idioms. Read your paragraph aloud.

© McGraw-Hill School Division

● **What's The Word?**

Match a clue to a time-order word or phrase. Write your answer.

tomorrow	today	first	before	next
happily ever after	never	last	yesterday	after
once upon a time	later	now	first	earlier

1. Fairy tales often begin with these words. _____

2. No matter how long you wait, this day never is today. _____

3. This means any time after right now. _____

4. This comes before second. _____

5. This rhymes with *cow* and is the opposite of *later*. _____

● **6.** This rhymes with *rafter* and is the opposite of *before*. _____

7. Not in the past. Not now. Not in the future. _____

8. A rebus for this word is [bee] + 4. _____

9. This is an antonym of the answer to number 3. _____

10. The one after this one is when? _____

11. This is the word for the phrase, *this day*. _____

12. To be at the head of the line is to be _____

13. This is an antonym of the answer to number 12. _____

14. This day is gone forever. _____

15. This is how fairy tales end. _____

© McGraw-Hill School Division

A Word Puzzle

Find the word or phrase that goes with each clue. Write each letter of your answer.

before	next	during	now	first
long ago	later	last	then	this morning

1. Now and   _ ☐ _ _

2. Many years past   _ ☐ _ _   _ _ _

3. Not before or later. Right   _ _ ☐

        T

4. Before anything else in time   _ ☐ _ _ _ _

5. In this early part of the day   _ _ _ _ ☐ _ _ _ _ _

6. Following right after this one   _ ☐ _ _

7. A moment earlier   _ _ ☐ _ _ _

8. Not now or earlier, but   ☐ _ _ _ _

9. At the same time as something else   _ _ _ ☐ _ _ _

        E

10. Finally   _ _ ☐ _

The letters in the boxes going down spell a common expression. What is it?

_____

© McGraw-Hill School Division

Using a Dictionary

Entry words in a dictionary are listed in **alphabetical order**. For words that begin with the same letter, look at the second letter. If the first two, or even three letters are the same, then look at the next letter.

A. Write each group of words in alphabetical order on the numbered lines .

maple **1.** _____

taper **2.** _____

define **3.** _____

condor **4.** _____

brace **5.** _____

paint **6.** _____

perch **7.** _____

event **8.** _____

eagle **9.** _____

pride **10.** _____

canoe **11.** _____

calf **12.** _____

card **13.** _____

cue **14.** _____

coat **15.** _____

loom **16.** _____

loft **17.** _____

local **18.** _____

live **19.** _____

loaf **20.** _____

© McGraw-Hill School Division

Go on

The dictionary can be divided into three parts or thirds. In the first third are words that begin with **a-f**. The middle third has words that begin with **g-p**, and the last third has words that begin with **q-z**.

B. Write each word under the correct part of the dictionary in alphabetical order.

offer	thermal	ankle	health	modem
yak	quit	frugal	wharf	judge
zone	enroll	lawyer	disk	chat

A-F

21. _____

22. _____

23. _____

24. _____

25. _____

G-P

26. _____

27. _____

28. _____

29. _____

30. _____

Q-Z

31. _____

32. _____

33. _____

34. _____

35. _____

© McGraw-Hill School Division

Using a Thesaurus

When should you use a thesaurus? Let's say you already know the meaning of a word. A **thesaurus** gives you a choice of other words with similar meanings that may work better in your sentence.

Entries in a thesaurus are in **alphabetical order**, just as they are in a dictionary. Sometimes a definition tells what each entry word and each synonym means.

before *adj.* at an earlier time; previously
▷ **beforehand** ahead of time
▷ **earlier** before the usual time
▷ **formerly** intime past; once
▷ **long ago** at a time in the far past
▷ **once** in a time now past

A. Write the answers to the following questions.

1. What is the entry word in the sample thesaurus on this page?

_____

2. What part of speech is *before*?

_____

3. Which synonym for *before* means "before the usual time?"

_____

4. Which synonym for *before* would you use to tell about things that happened in the past?

_____

5. Write the synonym for before that best completes this sentence:

Our school was _____ known as Hudson Street School.

© McGraw-Hill School Division

Using a thesaurus can help you find more interesting and exact words to make your writing better.

B. For each blank with an **A**, write a synonym for *after*. For each blank with a **B**, write a synonym for *before*. Use the thesaurus.

6.-15. My family has lived in many places._____
                                                                    B

we lived in New Jersey. _____ we moved to New York.
                                                    A

But _____ I was six-years old we have lived in Vermont.
                    A

_____ our house was a country schoolhouse.
              B

_____ it was almost falling down!_____
              B   A

we bought it and fixed it up to be a summer home. Two years

_____ we moved here to live all year round.
              A

_____ we have liked living here. But now we are
              B

getting tired of the long winters. "The winter seems to come

_____ every year," says Mom. They are talking about
              B

moving south. I wonder where we will live _____ ?
                                                          A

© McGraw-Hill School Division

Vocabulary: Compound Words

Compound words are words made from two or more words joined together. Often you can understand the meaning of a compound by looking at each word.

paintbrush =	brush for paint
sunflowers =	flowers like the sun
backyard =	a yard in the back
birdbath =	a bath for birds
watercolors =	paints for use with water

A. Find the compound word above that completes each sentence below. Write it on the line.

1. Audrey likes to paint with

_____ .

2. On warm days she likes to paint outside in her

_____ .

3. She sits at the picnic table and imagines a painting of the

_____ .

4. She dips her _____ into the water and wets her paper.

5. Today she will paint some beautiful yellow

_____ .

Go on

© McGraw-Hill School Division

B. Make a compound word. Draw a line to match each word in
Column **A** with a word in Column **B**.

	A	**B**	
6.	star	weed	_____
7.	bare	doors	_____
8.	out	fish	_____
9.	sea	shore	_____
10.	sea	foot	_____

C. Now use the new words you formed to complete the sentences.

11. Simon's family visits the _____

for vacation.

12. Simon likes to walk _____

on the beach.

13. The family often eats _____ .

14. At low tide, the rocks are slippery with green and brown

_____ .

15. In a tide pool, Simon once found a tiny

_____ .

© McGraw-Hill School Division

● # Multiple Meanings

Many words have more than one meaning. The meanings of some words also have changed over time. A dictionary will show different word meanings by numbering the definitions.

---

snowball *n.* **1.** a ball made of snow packed together
2. a shrub with clusters of large, rounded, white flowers
v. **1.** to throw snowballs at
2. to grow rapidly in size, as a rolling snowball does

● **A.** Read the dictionary entry above. Then write the definition of the underlined word in each sentence.

1. Hey! Who threw that <u>snowball</u> at me?

_____

2. The problems with the computer <u>snowballed</u> after 5 P.M.

_____

3. My brother's friends tried to <u>snowball</u> us when we left the house.

_____

4. Aunt Tessa has a huge <u>snowball</u> planted in front of her house.

_____

5. Which definition of *snowball* do you think is the oldest? Why?

_____

_____

© McGraw-Hill School Division

B. Read each sentence. Look up each of the underlined words in a
dictionary. Write the definition that tells how the word is used in
the sentence.

6. The problem with my computer was in the software, not the <u>hardware</u>.

_____

_____

7. Marisa's performance was the <u>keystone</u> that made the play a success.

_____

_____

8. We thought Joe gave a <u>lame</u> excuse for not helping.

_____

9. The mayor won the election by a <u>landslide</u>.

_____

10. The road was buried under the <u>landslide</u>.

_____

Writing Activity

Write a paragraph that explains how to use a machine you have in
your home. Then underline two or three words that have more than
one meaning. Ask a friend to tell you what other meanings the
words can have.

© McGraw-Hill School Division

Word Clues

Use the clues to find the correct words, and write them on the lines.

icecap	snowboard	carpool	hothouse

1. It's not a plant that grows houses, but a plant you grow indoors.

_ _ _ _ _ _ _ ☐ _

2. Its not a house that is too hot; it's a building for growing certain plants.

_ _ _ ☐ _ _ _

3. It's not a hat made of ice; it's a sheet of ice that covers the land.

_ _ _ _ _ _

4. You can't put a nail into this board, but you can ride it downhill in the snow.

☐ _ _ _ _ _ _ _ _

5. This doesn't conceal anything, but it covers the cow.

_ ☐ _ _ _ _ _

6. This wood can't bark, but it is a kind of tree.

_ _ _ ☐ _ _ _

7. It is not a house to keep your boat in, but a place to live.

_ _ _ ☐ _ _ _ _

8. You don't need to unlock this board.

_ ☐ _ _ _ _ _

9. It is not a place to take your car swimming; it's a group of people who share rides.

_ _ _   _ ☐ _ _

10. Unscramble the letters in the boxes to make a compound word.

_____

© McGraw-Hill School Division

Crossword Puzzle

yard sale	root word	snowdrop	evergreen	seaman
lawmaker	clubhouse	walkway	raceway	supermarket

Use the words to solve the puzzle.

Down

1. A place where a club meets.

3. Synonym for sailor.

4. A path or sidewalk.

5. A word that you can add a suffix to.

7. A type of tree that has needles instead of leaves.

Across

2. Someone who makes laws.

3. A small white flower that blooms in very early spring.

6. A large grocery store.

8. A sale that people have in their yards.

9. A place to hold a race.

© McGraw-Hill School Division

Using the Dictionary

> Each page in the dictionary has **guide words** in the top corner.
> The guide words show the first and last entry words on the page.
> If a word fits in alphabetical order between the guide words, it will
> be on that page.

---

baby/badger

baby *n.* **1.** a very young child **2.** a childish person
v. to treat like a baby
back *n.* the part of the body behind
the chest
v. to move backward
bad *adj.* **1.** having little worth **2.** not good; evil
badger *n.* a mammal with short legs and long claws
v. to bother with questions

A. Write the answers to the following questions.

1. What is the first entry word on the sample dictionary page?

_____

2. What is the last entry word on the page?

_____

3. What are the two guide words?

_____

4. Would base be an entry word on this page? Explain your answer.

_____

5. Why are guide words helpful?

_____

© McGraw-Hill School Division

B. Look at the sample guide words below. Write the words under the appropriate guide words.

sure	scabbard	scare	swallow	scribble
sunlight	scarlet	supple	save	suite
scoop	sulfur	suburb	suffrage	sausage

sauce/script   **submit/swan**

6. _____   13. _____

7. _____   14. _____

8. _____   15. _____

9. _____   16. _____

10. _____   17. _____

11. _____   18. _____

12. _____   19. _____

                                 20. _____

© McGraw-Hill School Division

Using a Thesaurus

> A **thesaurus** can help you improve your writing. Use a thesaurus when you need more interesting or more exact words to make your wording clear.

---

new *adj.* recently grown or made
▷ **young** in the early part of life
▷ **modern** up-to-date, not old fashioned
▷ **original** not thought of or heard before
▷ **different** not alike or similar
▷ **unfamiliar** not known before; strange
ANTONYM: **old; old-fashioned**

A. Write the answers to the following questions.

1. What is the entry word in the thesaurus sample?

_____

2. How many synonyms are listed for *new*?

_____

3. Which synonym could you substitute for *new* in this sentence:
*The spaceship's mission was to seek out **new** civilizations.*

_____

4. Which synonym for *new* is an antonym for "old-fashioned"?

_____

5. Which synonym could you substitute for *new* in this sentence:
*Jim came up with a **new** idea for a class project.*

_____

© McGraw-Hill School Division

B. Look up each **bold** type word in the thesaurus. Write a synonym for each word to make the sentence more interesting and exact.

The river otter lives near streams and rivers. Otters have (6) **wide** snouts, small ears, and (7) **little** legs with webbed feet and (8) **big** tails. Otters are (9) **good** swimmers and are very playful. They love to slide down mudbanks and snow banks and (10) **dive** into the water. Otters have (11) **thick** brown fur that keeps them warm even in (12) **cold** water.

Young otters are born in late winter and (13) **stay** with their parents in family groups until the second year. Otters have a (14) **large** territory and (15) **go** many miles in search of food.

6. _____

7. _____

8. _____

9. _____

10. _____

11. _____

12. _____

13. _____

14. _____

15. _____

Writing Activity

Make a list of five words to describe one of your friends. Then find each word in the thesaurus and choose a synonym which gives a more exact meaning to the description.

Vocabulary: Prefixes and Suffixes

A **prefix** is a word part that is added to the beginning of a root or base word to change its meaning.

Prefix	Meaning	Example
un-, dis-	not, the opposite of	unsure, distrust
re-	again, back	rewrite

A. Write the answers to the questions.

1. Which two prefixes mean "not" or "the opposite of?"

_____

2. What does it mean to *distrust* someone?

_____

3. What do you do if you rewrite your homework assignment?

_____

4. What does it mean to be unsure of something?

_____

5. Add a prefix to *visit* to make a word that means "visit again."

_____

© McGraw-Hill School Division

Go on

B. Add the prefix that is in parentheses to the root or base word and write the new word.

6. (re) read _____

7. (dis) agree _____

8. (dis) count _____

9. (un) truth _____

10. (un) usual _____

11. (dis) appeared_____

12. (un) happy_____

13.(re) appeared_____

14. (un) sure _____

15. (dis) obey _____

C. Choose from the words you wrote in Part B to complete the paragraph.

16.-20.   The book I read this week is a mystery. I was _____

how the story would end. One of the characters in the book_____

at the beginning. However, she _____ near the end

of the book. I didn't understand this part, so I _____

it. It is not _____ for me to read a book I really

like three or four times.

Writing Activity

Write a review of a book you would like others to read. Use as many words with prefixes as you can.

© McGraw-Hill School Division

Similes and Metaphors

Writers often use comparisons to make their writing more interesting, or to help make a point. A comparison says that something about one thing is like something about another thing.

A **simile** compares two things using the words *like* or *as*. A **metaphor** is a comparison that does not use *like* or *as*. It says something is something else.

Simile: *Joan is **as quick as lightning** when it comes to math.*
Simile: *Her mind works **like a computer**.*
Metaphor: *Leon is **a walking encyclopedia** about baseball.*

A. Write the answers to the questions.

1. In the first simile above, what is Joan being compared to?

_____

2. What is Joan's mind compared to in the second example?

_____

3. What do these two comparisons tell you about Joan's ability in math?

_____

4. In the third example, what is Leon being compared to?

_____

5. What does this comparison mean?

_____

© McGraw-Hill School Division

B. Read the following paragraph. Underline each metaphor or simile, and write it in the columns below.

6.-10. Eddie Vega is a real workhorse. If he is elected class president,

he will work like ten people for our class. Eddie is smart, too. He is a real

Einstein when it comes to solving problems. Ideas grow in his mind like

mushrooms. For a class president who is as dependable as heat in summertime,

vote for Eddie Vega.

Similes	Metaphors
6. _____	9. _____
7. _____	10. _____
8. _____	

Writing Activity

Write a paragraph to persuade someone to do something that you think is a good idea. Use similes and metaphors in your writing to help get your points across.

© McGraw-Hill School Division

Word Search

Look at each prefix. Use the clue and a word from the box to make a new word. Write the new word on the line, find it in the puzzle, and circle it.

read	important	clear	turn	honest
respect	obey	enter	wise	view

1. re-   to look at again _____

2. dis-   not obey _____

3. re-   enter again _____

4. un-   not important _____

5. un-   not wise _____

6. dis-   to not have respect _____

7. re-   go back _____

8. un-   not easily seen through _____

9. re-   read again _____

10. dis- not honest _____

```
C D I S R E S P E C T U
U A R O V I E D E D R N
B N C C A N O I P I S I
R S C Y O U T S I S R M
E N T L E N O H P O E P
C R E R E A D O R B V O
F I N D I A R N O E I R
R E E N T E R E S Y E T
T H E U N W I S E I W A
W O A S T R E T U R N N
E G A S S E M T M O U T
```

© McGraw-Hill School Division

Crossword Puzzle

Use the clues to solve the puzzle.

reedit	redo	unlikely	unlock	rewrite
renew	unlikely	dislodge	disobey	distrust

Across

1. To not trust someone
5. To break a rule or law
6. To do something again
7. To edit something again
8. Not probable; not likely

Down

1. To move or force out of place
2. Not true
3. To open something that was locked
4. To write over again
7. To make new or as if new again

© McGraw-Hill School Division

Using a Dictionary

> Prefixes are word parts added to a root or a base word to change its meaning. Many prefixes are in the **dictionary**. You often can find the meaning of a word with a prefix by looking up the meaning of the prefix and the meaning of the base word.
>
> **pre-** A prefix that means "before" or "ahead of time":
> *Prehistoric means before history was written down.*

A. Find the meaning of each base word and its prefix. Then write the meaning of the word.

1. antifreeze _____

2. postwar _____

3. preview _____

4. misbehave _____

5. nonfiction _____

Go on

© McGraw-Hill School Division

B. Look up the meaning of each prefix in the box. Add a prefix to the underlined base word to make a word that fits the definition. Write the new word.

mis-	in-	re-

6. not <u>active</u> _____

7. to <u>claim</u> again _____

8. to <u>understand</u> in the wrong way _____

9. not <u>complete</u> _____

10. to <u>turn</u> back _____

C. Write a word from Part B to complete each sentence below.

11. I used to be an active member of the club. Now I am on the

_____ list.

12. You didn't finish your test. You left some answers

_____ .

13. I want to stop at the library to

_____these books.

14. Did you _____what I meant?

15. Jim stopped at the lost and found to _____

his misplaced backpack.

© McGraw-Hill School Division

Using a Thesaurus

You can use a **thesaurus** to find synonyms for many words that have prefixes. You may have to first look up the base word and then add the prefix to the synonym. Prefixes such as *un-* or *dis-* will make the base word an antonym because they both mean "not."

unusual *adj.* not usual, common, or ordinary
▷ **different** not alike or similar
▷ **peculiar** not usual, strange; queer
▷ **rare** not often seen, happening or found
▷ **uncommon** not usually found or seen
ANTONYMS common, ordinary, usual

A. Write the answers.

1. Which synonym for *unusual* means "not alike or similar?"

_____

2. Which synonym means "not usually found or seen?"

_____

3. What antonyms are given for *unusual*?

_____

4. Which synonym could you use to replace *unusual* in this sentence:
The refrigerator had an <u>unusual</u> smell?

_____

5. Which synonym would you use to replace *unusual* in this sentence:
A bald eagle is still an unusual sight in many states?

_____

© McGraw-Hill School Division

B. Look up the underlined words in the thesaurus. Choose a synonym you
   could substitute for each and rewrite the sentence.

6. My two brothers are not twins, but they are <u>alike</u> in many ways.

   _____

   _____

7. I <u>dislike</u> having to weed the garden!

   _____

   _____

8. Shawn is <u>happy</u> that he is not moving after all.

   _____

   _____

9. I've never been on this road--it's completely <u>new</u> to me.

   _____

   _____

10. In the movie, the UFO glowed with a <u>strange</u> green light.

   _____

   _____

© McGraw-Hill School Division

Vocabulary: Synonyms and Antonyms

Synonyms are words that have the same or almost the same meaning.

cheerful • happy	gloomy • sad
pretty • lovely	angry • furious
cheap • inexpensive	hard • difficult

Antonyms are words that have opposite meanings.

old • new	cheerful • grumpy
hard • easy	stiff • flexible
tired • fresh	clean • dirty

A. Look at the underlined words in each sentence. Write whether the pairs are *synonyms* or *antonyms*.

1. Stanley is <u>skinny</u> and his brother Sid is also <u>slim</u>.

_____

2 I <u>like</u> eggplant, but I <u>hate</u> zucchini.

_____

3. This road is <u>narrow</u> here, although it is <u>broad</u> near the stores.

_____

4. While you <u>busy</u> yourself with schoolwork, I will <u>occupy</u> my time with reading.

_____

5. Can you tell whether his story is <u>true</u> or <u>false</u>?

_____

Go on →

© McGraw-Hill School Division

B. Write the synonym (**S**) or antonym (**A**) that completes each sentence.

plan	supplies	jumble	garments	neat

6. Jane's closet was a <u>mess</u>. She couldn't find anything

   in the _**S**_____ .

7. She decided to get rid of the <u>confusion</u> and make a _**A**_____ .

8. Jane put <u>clothes</u> she didn't wear anymore in a box. She would give

   these _**S**_____to charity.

9. She put her painting <u>tools</u> and her other art _**A**_____

   in a box on her bookshelf.

10. Jane worked hard to make her room <u>tidy</u>. She promised to keep it

    _**S**_____ from now on.

C. Use the clues or the thesaurus to write the answers.

11. A mountain might be described with this antonym

    for *low*. _____

12. This is a synonym for *funny*. _____

13. This word is both a synonym for *like* and a synonym for *love*. _____

14. This synonym for *nothing* is also a number. _____

15. This antonym of *brave* is a synonym of *frightened*. _____

Writing Activity

Write a paragraph explaining how to play a game or a sport.
Use antonyms in your writing to show clear contrasts.

© McGraw-Hill School Division

● Word Choice

Synonyms are words that have the same or almost the same meanings.

　　　walk • march • amble　　　　　angry • furious • enraged

Some synonyms have different **shades of meaning.**

　March means to walk rhythmically in a purposeful way.

　Amble means to walk slowly or leisurely.
　Someone who is *furious* or *enraged* is more than merely *angry*.

You can use synonyms to make your writing clearer and more precise.

A. Write the answers. Use the thesaurus.

1. If you were showing off, would you *strut* or would you *amble*?

_____

2. You could describe a slim person as *slender* or as *scrawny*. Which word is a compliment?

_____

3. Which word shows a deeper feeling, *glad* or *thrilled*?

_____

4. Which word would you use to describe the smell of a pleasant scent, *aroma* or *stench*?

_____

5. You might describe a person who does not like to spend money as *thrifty* or as *stingy*. Which word makes the person sound wise?

_____

© McGraw-Hill School Division

Go on ➡

B. Annie wants to revise a paragraph that she wrote. Help her change the tone by choosing more precise words. Choose an antonym or a synonym for each underlined word and rewrite the paragraph. When you are finished, compare your revision with a classmate's.

6.-15. At the edge of my town there is a large house that belongs to Mrs. Summer. There are big windows in the front of the house and a plain front door. Behind the house there is a large area with a picnic table. There is also a nice garden with a small pond. My neighbor grows many good vegetables and pretty flowers in her garden.

cottage	mansion	cabin	tiny
spacious	ugly	inedible	delicious
simple	narrow	elegant	deck
patio	wonderful	lovely	tasty
enormous	huge	miniature	disgusting

_____

_____

_____

_____

_____

_____

Writing Activity

Write a description of a place you know well. Underline some of the nouns, verbs, and adjectives. Then revise the description, substituting more colorful synonyms for the underlined words. Read both descriptions to a classmate. Which version did he or she prefer?

© McGraw-Hill School Division

Word Search

Use the clues to find the correct words, and write them on the lines. Then find and circle the words in the puzzle. Words in the puzzle may go across, down, or diagonally.

faithful	swollen	often	crisp	neat
tiny	serious	aroma	peculiar	exhausted

1. This word is a synonym for *odd*. _____

2. This is an antonym for *limp*. _____

3. This word is an antonym for *enormous*. _____

4. This word means "pleasing smell." _____

5. This word is a synonym for *tired*. _____

6. This word is an antonym for *shrunken*. _____

7. This is a synonym for *tidy*. _____

8. This word means "frequently." _____

9. This word is the opposite of *lighthearted* or *silly*. _____

10. This word is a synonym for *symbol*. _____

```
S H E C S O F T E N C S
W E N A R O M A I U R E
O L E S A I T S O N A R
L L A P R M S E I R Y I
L O T R T O C P H G N O
E X H A U S T E D B N U
N O P E C U L I A R T S
```

© McGraw-Hill School Division

Crossword Puzzle

Use the words to solve the puzzle.

deliver	action	idea	star	elaborate
tired	amble	pennant	ancient	detest

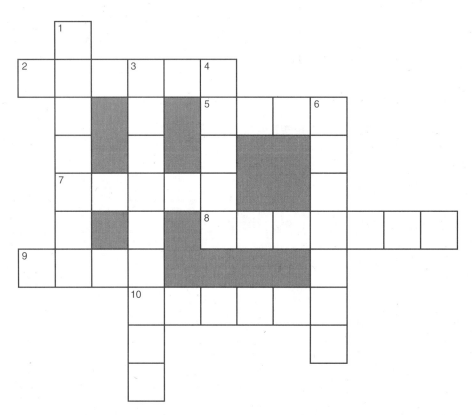

Across
2. Synonym for *dislike*.
5. Synonym for *thought*.
7. Synonym for *stroll*.
8. Synonym for *bring*.
9. Synonym for *celebrity*.
10. Antonym for *idleness*.

Down
1. Synonym for *flag*.
3. Antonym for *simple*.
4. Antonym for *fresh*.
6. Antonym for *modern*.

© McGraw-Hill School Division

Using a Dictionary

Entry words often have more than one **definition**, or meaning. Sometimes the definition will include a single word. This word is a synonym. Other definitions of the word mean something else.

Look at the entries for *cold* and *crank*.

cold 1. Having a low temperature.
2. Feeling a lack of warmth; chilly.
3. Not friendly or kind. *Adjective*
1. A lack of warmth or heat
2. A common sickness that causes sneezing, coughing, and a running or stuffy nose. *Noun*

crank 1. A part of a machine with a handle attached to a rod. When the handle is turned, the rod turns with it. *Noun*
2. A person with strange ideas.
3. Someone who is always grouchy or cross. *Noun*

A. Write the answers.

1. What synonym is given for *cold*?

_____

2. Write the definition of *cold* that makes it a synonym for *flu* or *virus*.

_____

3. Which definition of *cold* makes it an antonym for *hot*?

_____

4. Write the definition of *cold* that is a synonym for *unfriendly*.

_____

5. Is a synonym given as one of the definitions of *crank* ?

_____

© McGraw-Hill School Division

B. Use a dictionary to find a synonym for the underlined word in each sentence.

6. It was a fine, crisp autumn day.

_____

7. We took a walk in the forest, but we lost the trail.

_____

8. We had to creep through the bushes on our hands and knees.

_____

9. Our shoes got muddy and our knees were dirty.

_____

10. We walked a long way before we found the path again.

_____

C. Write the definitions.

11. The definition of *angry* that is a synonym for *hurtful* is _____ .

_____

12. The definition of *cheap* that is an antonym for *expensive* is _____ .

_____

13. The definition of *fiery* that is an antonym for *calm* is _____ .

_____

14. The definition of *modern* that is an antonym of *old-fashioned* is _____ .

_____

15. The definition of *still* that is a synonym for *soundless* is _____ .

_____

© McGraw-Hill School Division

Using a Thesaurus

A **thesaurus** is a reference source you can use to find synonyms, and sometimes antonyms, for many common words. Entries in a thesaurus are in alphabetical order, just as entries in a dictionary.

nice *adj.* agreeable or pleasing
▷ **gentle** mild and kindly in manner.
▷ **kind** friendly; good-hearted.
▷ **pleasant** agreeable; giving pleasure to.
▷ **sweet** agreeable.
ANTONYM: mean

A. Write the answers to the following questions.

1. What is the entry word in the sample thesaurus on this page?

   _____

2. What part of speech is *nice*?

   _____

3. Which synonym could you substitute for *nice* in the following sentence:
   We had a nice time at Aunt Marie's house.

   _____

4. Which synonym for *nice* means "good-hearted?"

   _____

5. Which word means the opposite of *nice*?

   _____

Go on

© McGraw-Hill School Division

B. Rewrite each sentence. Use the thesaurus in this book to replace each underlined word with a more exact synonym.

6. We decided to <u>ask</u> for information at the front desk of the hotel.

_____

7. The museum featured a display of <u>old</u> jewelry.

_____

8. Unfortunately for our plans, the weather forecast was not <u>right</u>.

_____

9. Tad could not <u>believe</u> how the visit would end.

_____

10. We stared in wonder at the baby's <u>small</u> fingers and toes.

_____

11. Our class <u>asked</u> permission from the principal to hold a book fair in the gym.

_____

12. I thought the movie was <u>awful</u>.

_____

13. When I am nervous I sometimes <u>laugh</u>.

_____

14. We <u>looked</u> at the beautiful painting for a long time.

_____

15. It's a beautiful day—let's go for a <u>walk</u> on the beach.

_____

© McGraw-Hill School Division

McGraw-Hill Language Arts
Grade 4, Unit 4 / 15

Vocabulary: Homophones and Homographs

Homophones are words that sound alike, but are spelled differently. They have different meanings, too.

road, rode   *know, no*

Homographs are words that are spelled alike, but are usually pronounced differently and have different meanings.

I gave Yolanda a <u>present</u> for her birthday.

The mayor will <u>present</u> the citizenship awards.

A. Write the answers to the questions.

1. What makes *road* and *rode* homophones?

_____

_____

2 Which word, *road* or *rode*, would you use in this sentence?

Bettina ____ her pony to school. _____

3. Name another homophone for *road* and *rode*. (Hint: It has something

to do with a boat.) _____

4. What makes *present* and *present* homographs?

_____

_____

5. If you are have knowledge about something, do you "no it"?

_____

© McGraw-Hill School Division

B. Underline the pair of homophones in each sentence. Then write both
words on the line.

6. A hungry and tired knight stayed here for the night._____

7. He had traveled for four long days._____

8. He hoped the wound on his heel would heal quickly.

_____

9. All the knight had to eat was a pair of apples and a pear.

_____

10. He had hoped to meet a deer so that he could have some meat.

_____

C. Look at the homograph in each sentence. Read the two meanings for
the word. Then circle the one that makes sense in the sentence and
write the letter on the line.

11. Mom reminded me to close the door. _____

    a. to shut   **b.** to bring together

12. We hired a man to haul away the refuse. _____

    a. garbage   **b.** to say no to

13. Please wind this loose yarn into a ball. _____

    a. moving air   **b.** to wrap something around something else

14. When you finish your song, take a bow. _____

    a. to bend at the waist   **b.** a knot with two or more loops

15. How long did it take for the wound to heal? _____

    a. past tense of wind   **b.** a cut or bruise

Writing Activity

Write a paragraph that uses at least four pairs of homophones
or homographs. Ask a friend to proofread your paragraph to
see if you used the homophones correctly.

© McGraw-Hill School Division

● Onomatopoeia

Onomatopoeia means forming a word by imitating the sound a thing makes. Look at the following sentence.

The cat meowed as the doorbell clanged.

Meowed and *clanged* and are examples of onomatopoeia.

There are many words in the English language which describe sounds. Writers sometimes make up their own words to describe sounds and to make their writing more colorful.

A. Underline the words in the paragraph which use onomatopoeia. Then write the words on the lines.

One afternoon we spread our blanket in the grass by the pond. We must have disturbed a little green snake sunning himself on a rock. He hissed at us before he slithered away. It was so quiet we could hear the lazy buzzing of bumblebees in the wildflowers. Far overhead there was the keer-keer of a hawk. Ashley tossed a pebble into the pond and it hit the water with a loud kerplunk. Then we both laughed when a frog startled us with a loud splash.

1. _____

2. _____

3. _____

4. _____

5. _____

© McGraw-Hill School Division

B. Help Sam, the sound-effects man. Someone took all the labels off his sound tapes. Match the words or phrases below with a word which describes the sound. Write the word on the line. Use a dictionary if you need help.

squish	slurp	honk	chirp	gurgle
murmur	clang	rustle	ding dong	who-whooo

6. loud alarm bell _____

7. water going down a drain _____

8. voices speaking quietly _____

9. walking in dry leaves _____

10. car horn _____

11. door bell _____

12. small bird _____

13. an owl's call _____

14. stepping in mud _____

15. drinking the last two drops of soda through a straw _____

Writing Activity

Make a list of five sounds you hear everyday. Think of a word (or make up a word) that describes the sound. Then read the sound words aloud to a friend and ask what activity or object the words describe.

© McGraw-Hill School Division

Riddle Time

Write a pair of homophones on the blanks to form an answer for each riddle.
The underlined words will give you clues. Use a dictionary if you need help
using the homophones correctly.

lone/loan	pain/pane	dew/due	desert/dessert	heard/herd
nose/knows	male/mail	bore/boar	need/knead	blue/blew

1. I am an <u>ache</u> in a <u>sheet of glass</u>.

I'm a _____ in a _____ .

2. I 'm a <u>man</u> that just came from the <u>post office</u>.

I'm a _____ with the _____ .

3. Don't <u>leave</u> before this <u>sweet treat</u>.

Don't _____ before _____ .

4. I am a <u>solitary</u> <u>gift of money</u> you have to pay back.

I'm a _____   _____ .

5. I am a <u>part of your face</u> that has <u>wisdom</u>.

I'm a _____ that _____ .

6. I am the <u>moisture</u> you <u>expect</u> to be on the grass.

I am the _____ that is _____ .

7. I am the <u>color</u> you turned when you <u>played the horn</u>.

You were _____ when you _____ .

8. Do you <u>tire</u> of this <u>wild pig</u>?

Does this _____   _____ you?

9. <u>Did you hear</u> about the <u>bunch of cows</u>?

Have you _____ of this _____ ?

10. What the baker <u>must do</u> to the bread <u>dough</u>.

He _____ to _____ it.

© McGraw-Hill School Division

Scrambled Eggs

Help the chef unscramble these eggs. Unscramble the letters in each egg to form a pair of homophones. Write the words on the lines. The sentence under each egg will give you a clue to one of the words in each pair.

1.

PEEEEACCIP

_____

_____

Just one portion.

2.

WEAYIHGW

_____

_____

How heavy is it?

3.

ATEGHEIT

_____

_____

It's a number less than 10.

4.

CCOOAURRSSEE

_____

_____

It's not smooth.

5.

BRBARAEEKK

_____

_____

A glass might do this.

6.

LOWFLRREOUF

_____

_____

You need it to bake.

© McGraw-Hill School Division

Using a Dictionary

A **dictionary** can help you find the meanings of homophones and homographs. Some dictionaries will list homophones of an entry word. Homographs usually have separate, numbered entries.

bass[1] **1.** The lowest man's singing voice.
2. A musical instrument with a similar range.
Another word that sounds like this is base.
bass (bās)
bass[2] Any of a number of North American fish
bass (bas)

knew Past tense of *know*.
Other words that sound like this are *gnu* and *new*.
knew (nü *or* nū)*verb*.

A. Write the answers to the following questions.

1. Write the meanings of *bass*[1]?

_____

2. Which entry, *bass*[1] or *bass*[2], is a homophone for *base*?

_____

3. What words are given as homophones of *knew*?

_____

4. Look up *gnu* in the dictionary. What is a gnu?

_____

5. Write *gnu* or *knew* or *new* on the lines to complete this sentence:

The zookeeper _____ the gentle _____

_____ would not hurt him.

Go on

B. Look up each underlined word in the dictionary. Write the meaning of the word as it is used in the sentence.

6. We turned on the television as we were finishing our evening meal.

_____

7. "Put on the weather channel," said Dad.

_____

8. The forecast came on as we started to eat dessert.

_____

9. The weather forecaster's face wore a grave expression.

_____

10. "Temperatures are well above the mean temperature for this time of year," he announced.

_____

11. "Record-breaking temperatures have caused many storms."

_____

12. "In Kansas, there was a severe hail storm."

_____

13. "A hurricane is forming near the Florida Keys," he added.

_____

14. "We can expect relief from the heat when cold air currents arrive."

_____

15. "The spring rains are expected in desert areas of the Southwest," he concluded.

_____

© McGraw-Hill School Division

Using a Thesaurus

> A **thesaurus** is a reference source you can use to find synonyms,
> and sometimes antonyms, for many common words. Like a dictionary,
> the entry words in a thesaurus are in alphabetical order. Guide words at
> the top of each page tell you the first and last entry words on the page.
>
> **gravel/groove**
> **great** *adj.* of unusual quality, ability, or quantity
> ▷ **remarkable;** having unusual qualities
> ▷ **superb;** greater ability than most
> ▷ **huge:** extremely large
> ▷ **important;** having great value or meaning
> ANTONYMS: little, small

A. Write the answers.

1. What are the guide words on this sample thesaurus page?

   _____

2. Which of these words would be found on this page: *guilt*, *gravity*,
   grease, *ground*?

   _____

3. What part of speech is *great*?

   _____

4. Which synonym could you substitute for *great* in this sentence?
   *Marie Curie made a **great** contribution to science.*

   _____

5. Write the homophone for *great* and define it.

   _____

© McGraw-Hill School Division

B. Look up the underlined words in the thesaurus. Then write answers.

6. Which synonym for _bare_ could you use to describe a room?

_____

7. Which synonym for _asked_ could you use in the following sentence?
"Oh, please? Pretty please?" baby asked.

_____

8. Which synonym for _look_ is a homophone for stair?

_____

9. Write the synonym for _know_ in this sentence:
I didn't know Uncle Bill without his beard.

_____

10. Which synonym for _groom_ would you use to describe caring for
a horse?

_____

11. Which synonym for _heart_ means the central, deepest part of something?

_____

12. Write the synonym for _disturb_ which is a homophone for *medal* and
could be used in this sentence: *I didn't want to ___ in his business.*

_____

13. Which synonym for _huge_ is a homophone for *grate*?

_____

14. Which synonym for _show_ is also a homograph and can be used in this
sentence: *The scientist was asked to _show_ evidence that her theory is
correct*?

_____

15. Write the synonym for _problem_ that is a homophone for *maize* and
fits this sentence: *We had so many choices and things to decide,
we felt we were lost in a _____.*

_____

© McGraw-Hill School Division

Vocabulary: Suffixes

A **suffix** is a word part that is added to the end of a base word or a root word to change its meaning.

Suffix	Meaning	Example
-er, -or	one who ___	painter, sailor
-less	without	meaningless
-able	able to be or do	breakable
-ly	in a ___ way	quickly
-ful	full of	joyful

A. Write the answers to the questions.

1. Which two suffixes mean "one who does (something)?"

   _____

2 If *-less* means "without," what does *meaningless* mean?

   _____

3. Which suffix has the opposite meaning of *-less*?

   _____

4. What word could you make that is an antonym of *meaningless*?

   _____

5. If something is said to be <u>breakable</u>, what does this mean?

   _____

© McGraw-Hill School Division

Go on

B. Add the suffix that is in parentheses to the base word and write the new word. Remember to make spelling changes if you need to. You may use a dictionary.

6. run (-er) _____

7. stress (-ful) _____

8. success (-ful) _____

9. wise (-ly) _____

10. poor (-ly) _____

C. Choose from the words you wrote in **B** to complete the paragraph.

11.-15.   Kira is the fastest _____ on our team.

But two days before the race she ran _____. It was

her worst time ever!

     Kira was worried. "I'm afraid I won't run well in the race," she said. "I need

more practice."

     Our coach gave her some good advice. "Don't run at all tomorrow,"

he said _____. "Just get lots of rest. Race day will be

_____. But just relax and you will

be_____."

Writing Activity

Think of two friends you have who have different personalities.
For instance, one might be a very upbeat, cheerful person.
The other might be more serious. Write a paragraph to
compare your two friends. Use words that contain sufffixes in
your comparison.

© McGraw-Hill School Division

● Root Words

> Many words in English are made up of word parts that come from Latin and Greek. If you know what these word parts mean, you can figure out many new words. For instance, *cyclo* is a **root word** that comes from Greek and means "ring." *Circ* is a root word that comes from Latin and also means "ring."
>
> *circ* means ring   *voc* means call or voice   *tain* means hold
>
> *cyclo* means ring   *spect* means to look at   *tract* means pull

A. Write the words on the lines next to their definitions.

1. A three-wheeled vehicle

_____

2. A machine often used to pull things

_____

3. To look into

_____

4. A show originally held in a large, circular space

_____

5. Expressed by the voice

_____

vocal
circus
inspect
tricycle
tractor

Go on ➡

© McGraw-Hill School Division

B. Underline the words that contain the word parts *circ*, *cyclo*, *spect*, *voc*, *tain*, or *tract*. Then follow the directions below.

6.-10. Our class has been learning to respect the environment. We decided to get the whole school involved in a recycling project. First, we set up several large containers in the lunchroom for bottles and plastics. Next, we circulated a newsletter, explaining what we were doing. Then, we made up a contract for our schoolmates to sign. Everyone promised to participate.

Now list the words you underlined and write their definitions.
Use a dictionary if you need help.

11. _____

12. _____

13. _____

14. _____

15. _____

Writing Activity

Think of other words you know which include the word parts *circ*, *cyclo*, *spect*, *voc*, *tain*, or *tract*. Check a dictionary to be sure you know what the words mean. Then write a paragraph using at least three words which contain *irc*, *cyclo*, *spect*, *voc*, *tain*, or *tract*.

© McGraw-Hill School Division

A Tale of Suffixes

These fish have lost their tails! Help them find the right tails by matching the word at the left with the suffix at the right. Draw a line between the fish and the correct tail. Then write the word, making spelling changes if you need to.

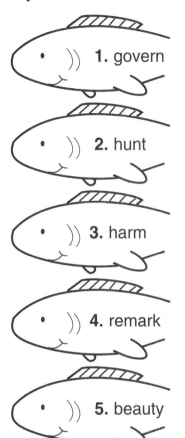

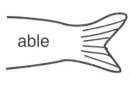 **1.** govern   able   _____

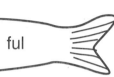 **2.** hunt   ful   _____

 **3.** harm   er   _____

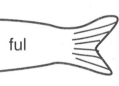 **4.** remark   ful   _____

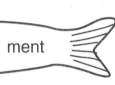 **5.** beauty   ment   _____

B. Now use the words from Part A to complete the sentences.

6.-10. The bald eagle is our national symbol. But this _____

bird almost became extinct. Sometimes a _____ would

shoot one by mistake. But the biggest problem was from a pesticide called

DDT. After scientists realized how _____ it was, the

_____ made laws against the use of DDT. Now the bald

eagle has made a _____ comeback.

© McGraw-Hill School Division

Word Search

Some words with suffixes are hidden in the puzzle. Use the clues below to find the words. Circle them in the puzzle and write the words on the lines.

C	A	R	E	L	E	S	S	L	B	T	A
D	V	M	O	N	T	H	L	Y	R	I	P
A	I	P	O	T	R	A	C	T	O	R	A
N	P	T	A	E	A	P	O	A	N	E	I
C	T	R	A	R	N	P	S	I	O	L	N
E	S	B	N	S	T	I	N	U	W	E	T
R	E	A	D	A	B	L	E	L	G	S	E
A	N	G	R	I	L	Y	Y	O	S	S	R

1. In an angry way _____

2. Not completely _____

3. Able to be read easily _____

4. Someone who dances _____

5. Someone who paints _____

6. Happening once a month _____

7. Not taking good care _____

8. In a happy way _____

9. Without tiring _____

10. A farm machine used to pull things _____

© McGraw-Hill School Division

Using a Dictionary

A dictionary can help you say an unfamiliar word. A dictionary entry shows the words divided into **syllables** and shows the pronunciation in a respelling with special symbols.

When a word has several syllables, part of the word is said with more stress. The accent mark in the respelling shows you which syllable to say with more stress.

agreeable 1. Nice; pleasant 2. Willing to give permission.
a•gree•a•ble (ə grē′ ə bəl)

A. Write the answers to the questions.

1. Write *agreeable* in syllables, as it is shown in the dictionary.

_____

2. How many syllables does *agreeable* have?

_____

3. Which syllable of *agreeable* is said with more stress?

_____

4. What symbol stands for the vowel sound in the first syllable?

_____

5. How does seeing a word divided into syllables help you with a new word?

_____

© McGraw-Hill School Division

Go on

B. Look up the following words in the dictionary. Write the words in syllables. Show the accent mark.

6. fearless _____

7. harmful _____

8. joyful _____

9. walker _____

10. porter _____

11. washable _____

12. calmly _____

13. agreement _____

14. sailor _____

15. cheerful _____

C. Underline the words that contain the suffixes *-er*, *-or*, *-ly*, *-ful*, *-less*, or *-able*. Then write each word on a line and show its syllables. Circle the syllable in each word that has the most stress.

16.-20.   Duke Ellington was a jazz musician and an orchestra leader. From

1927 to 1931, he and his orchestra played in New York City at The Cotton

Club in Harlem. But Ellington is probably best known as a remarkable

composer. He wrote movie scores, several long pieces for orchestra and

soloists, over one thousand short pieces, and had countless hits.

21. _____

22. _____

23. _____

24. _____

25. _____

© McGraw-Hill School Division

Using a Thesaurus

The suffix **-ly** means *in a ___ way*. Words that end in *-ly* are usually **adverbs**, words used to describe how something is done. You can use a thesaurus to find synonyms for many adverbs. For some words you will have to look up the base word and then add the suffix to it.

loudly *adv.* in a loud way
▷ **noisily** in a loud, harsh, way
quiet *adj.* with little or no noise
▷ **calm** without excitement or strong feeling
▷ **humble** modest; not proud
▷ **still** without sound or motion
ANTONYMS: loud, noisy, excited

A. Write the answers.

1. Substitute a word for *loudly* in the following sentence. Write the word.
The children chattered <u>loudly</u> *as they boarded the bus.*

_____

2. What part of speech are most words that end with the suffix *-ly*?

_____

3. What suffix could you add to the word *quiet* to complete the sentence below? Write the new word.

Dad spoke _____*because the baby was asleep.*

4. Which word in the thesaurus sample means the same as "not proud?"

_____

5. Which synonym could you substitute for *quietly* in this sentence:
The man did his good deeds <u>quietly</u>, *without bragging about them*?

_____

 Go on

© McGraw-Hill School Division

B. Look up the underlined words in the thesaurus. Choose a synonym you could substitute for each and rewrite the sentence. You may have to add a suffix to the base word.

6. Marta's fingers were <u>quick</u> as she plucked the guitar strings.

_____

_____

7. Thomas leaped <u>gracefully</u> over the hurdles.

_____

_____

8. Anita's <u>quick</u> mind solved the complicated problem in record time.

_____

_____

9. We motioned <u>quietly</u> to Tessa not to let on that she saw us.

_____

_____

10. The soldier was given a medal for acting bravely during the battle.

_____

_____

© McGraw-Hill School Division

What Is a Thesaurus?

A **thesaurus** is a reference source you can use to find synonyms, and sometimes antonyms, for many common words. **Synonyms** are words that mean the same or almost the same thing. **Antonyms** are words that have opposite meanings. Use a thesaurus when you are looking for a more interesting or more exact word. Read this sentence:

> *The sunset was pretty.*

If you check the word pretty in the thesaurus, you will find these words: *attractive*, *beautiful*, and *gorgeous*. One of these words will make your sentence more interesting and precise.

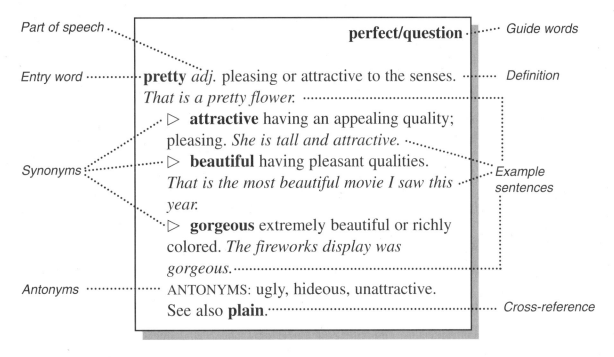

Part of speech

Entry word

Synonyms

Antonyms

Guide words

Definition

Example sentences

Cross-reference

perfect/question

pretty *adj.* pleasing or attractive to the senses. *That is a pretty flower.*
  ▷ **attractive** having an appealing quality; pleasing. *She is tall and attractive.*
  ▷ **beautiful** having pleasant qualities. *That is the most beautiful movie I saw this year.*
  ▷ **gorgeous** extremely beautiful or richly colored. *The fireworks display was gorgeous.*
ANTONYMS: ugly, hideous, unattractive.
See also **plain**.

- The **guide words** at the top of each page show the first and last word on that page.

- The word *pretty* is the entry word.

- The **part of speech** of each entry is given.

- A **definition** tells what the entry word and each synonym mean.

- An **example sentence** helps you to use each entry word and each synonym.

- A **cross-reference** sends you to additional information.

© McGraw-Hill School Division

A

above *prep.* over or higher than. *The kite flew above the trees.*
▷ **over** in a place or position higher than. *Clouds drifted over the city.*
ANTONYMS: See also **below**.

after *prep.* following in place; behind. *I was after Joey in the line.*
▷ **later** after the usual time. *We stayed at the party later than we'd planned.*
▷ **next** immediately afterward. *March is the next month after February.*
▷ **since** from a particular time in the past until now. *We have not seen Sammy since he moved to Florida.*
▷ **then** after that; next. *First we went for a swim, then we ate our lunch.*

agree *v.* to say one is willing. *I agree to clean my room every Saturday.*
▷ **approve** to agree to officially. *The committee will approve the use of music in the cafeteria.*
▷ **consent** to say yes. *I consent to your plan.*
ANTONYMS: refuse, reject, disagree

alike *adj.* like one another. *No two snowflakes are ever exactly alike.*
▷ **same** like another in every way. *The twins always dress in the same way.*
▷ **similar** having many qualities that are the same. *These two coats are similar.*

allow See also **let**.

always *adv.* as long as possible. *I will remember their kindness always.*
▷ **continually** without stop. *My tooth aches continually.*
▷ **forever** for all time. *Ned will be my friend forever.*
ANTONYMS: never, rarely, seldom

angry *adj.* feeling or showing anger. *Don's remark made me angry.*
▷ **enraged** filled with rage; angry beyond control. *The enraged lion growled loudly.*
▷ **furious** extremely angry. Marty was furious when he found out I ruined his bike.

answer *v.* to give a spoken or written response. *I wonder whether Celia is going to answer my letter.*
▷ **reply** to say in response. *If he insults you, don't reply. Just walk away.*
▷ **respond** to give an answer. James did not respond to my question.
ANTONYMS: See also **ask**.

ask *v.* to put a question to. *Let's ask for directions.*
▷ **inquire** to seek information by asking questions. *Please inquire at the desk.*
▷ **question** to try to get information (from someone). *Bill's mother questioned him about where he had been.*
ANTONYMS: See also **answer**.

© McGraw-Hill School Division

awful *adj.* causing fear, dread, or awe. *The tree made an awful noise when it fell.*

▷ **dreadful** causing great fear. *I am in shock from the dreadful experience.*

▷ **horrible** causing or tending to cause horror. *What a horrible sight!*

▷ **terrible** causing terror or awe. *Jason received some terrible news.*

▷ **unpleasant** not pleasant. *Camping in the rain was an unpleasant experience.*

ANTONYMS: pleasant, wonderful

B

bare *adj.* without clothing or covering. *We wriggled our bare feet in the water.*

▷ **empty** having nothing or no one in it. *Mom washed out the empty vase.*

▷ **plain** without decoration. *Susannah wore a plain white dress.*

battle *n.* a fierce contest between people or groups. *The football game was a real battle.*

▷ **conflict** a strong disagreement. *The two sides are in a bitter conflict over the issue.*

▷ **struggle** a contest of power or skill. *The struggle between the teams ended in a tie.*

beautiful *adj.* full of beauty; having qualities that are pleasing. *What a beautiful sunset!*

▷ **attractive** pleasing to the eye. *The store has an attractive entrance.*

▷ **lovely** beautiful in a comforting way. *This is a lovely day.*

▷ **pretty** pleasing or attractive, often said of something small and dainty. *What pretty flowers these are!*

ANTONYMS: ugly, unattractive

before *adv.* at an earlier time; previously

▷ **beforehand** ahead of time. *Let's check beforehand what time the movie begins.*

▷ **earlier** before the usual time. *Winter seemed to come earlier this year.*

▷ **formerly** in time past; once. *People formerly depended on horses and wagons for transportation.*

▷ **long ago** at a time in the far past. *Long ago, people cooked all their meals at a fireplace.*

▷ **once** in a time now past. *Once the main street of our town was a dirt road.*

believe *v.* to think something is true. *Do you believe he is telling the truth?*

▷ **accept** to take as truth. *He hoped she would accept his version of the events.*

▷ **be convinced** to be persuaded. *Lu needs to be convinced that the plan is good.*

▷ **imagine** to suppose; guess. *I don't imagine we'll have a picnic if it rains.*

▷ **suppose** to believe; guess. *I suppose I'll finish my homework soon.*

© McGraw-Hill School Division

▷ **think** to have or form an opinion. *I think we should leave before it gets dark.*
ANTONYMS: doubt, reject

below *prep.* lower than in place, rank, or value. *The small plane flew beneath the clouds.*

▷ **beneath** lower than; under. *We planted daffodils beneath the tree.*

▷ **under** in or to a place lower than. *The letter was under a pile of books.*
ANTONYMS: See also **above**.

big *adj.* of great size. *Do you have any big boxes?*

▷ **enormous** much greater than the usual size. *There is an enormous spider in the bathtub.*

▷ **giant** very large. *A redwood is a giant tree.*

▷ **gigantic** like a giant; huge and powerful. *The gigantic crane easily lifted the truck.*

▷ **huge** extremely big. *That huge man plays football.*

▷ **large** of great size. *Paula seldom has a large lunch.*

▷ **wide** covering a large area from side to side. *The doorway to the gym is very wide.*
ANTONYMS: See also **little**.

brave *adj.* willing to face danger; without fear. *The brave firefighter raced into the burning house.*

▷ **bold** showing courage; fearless. *The bold explorer went where no one else had ever gone.*

▷ **courageous** having courage. *A courageous woman dove into the icy water to save the child.*

▷ **daring** willing to take risks. *The daring princess escaped from the tower.*

▷ **fearless** without fear. *The fearless explorer entered the thick jungle.*
ANTONYMS: afraid, fearful

break *v.* to come apart; to separate into pieces. *These glass animals break easily.*

▷ **crack** to break without fully separating. *The crack on the shell means the eggs are ready to hatch.*

▷ **fracture** to break or split a bone. *Juan fractured his ankle and had to leave the game.*

▷ **shatter** to break suddenly into many pieces. *The vase will shatter if you drop it.*

bright *adj.* filled with light; shining. *Is that light bright enough to read by?*

▷ **brilliant** shining or sparkling with light. *The crown was decorated with brilliant gems.*

▷ **shiny** shining; bright. *Her blue coat has shiny silver buttons.*
ANTONYMS: dark, dull

build *v.* to put together parts and material. *They built the tree house yesterday.*

▷ **make** to build or prepare. *Andrea made the salad.*

© McGraw-Hill School Division

▷ **construct** to put up. *The school was constructed in 1912.*
ANTONYMS: to tear down, wreck, demolish

— C —

careful *adj.* done with close attention. *She made a careful check of the electric wires.*
▷ **cautious** using close care. *Sally was cautious when she walked across the narrow bridge.*
▷ **detailed** dealing with all the little parts of something. *The model came with detailed instructions.*
▷ **thorough** leaving nothing out; careful and complete. *Please do a thorough job of cleaning the desk.*
ANTONYMS: careless, sloppy

cave *n.* a natural hollow space in a mountain. *Bears sleep in a cave for the winter.*
▷ **burrow** a hole in the ground made by an animal for shelter. *The rabbits lived in a burrow.*
▷ **cavern** a large cave, often underground. *We explored a cavern deep in the ground.*

clean *adj.* free from dirt. *Max took the clean clothes out of the washing machine.*
▷ **pure** not stained, dirty, or mixed with anything. *We drank pure water from a spring.*
▷ **spotless** absolutely clean. *His new shirt was spotless.*
ANTONYMS: dirty, filthy

cold *adj.* having a low temperature. *The desert has hot days and cold nights.*
▷ **chilly** uncomfortably cool. *The first day was wet and chilly.*
▷ **freezing** extremely cold. *Our hands were numb from the freezing cold.*
▷ **frigid** very cold. *The winters in northern Minnesota are often frigid.*
▷ **icy** very cold. *An icy wind stung our cheeks.*
ANTONYMS: See also **hot**.

collect *v.* to gather or bring (things) together. *Tom collected soda cans to raise money.*
▷ **assemble** to gather or bring together, especially people. *The mayor assembled the council.*
▷ **compile** to collect and put together (information), as in a list or report. *Nancy compiled a list of members.*
▷ **gather** to bring together in one place or group. *Ray gathered all the team members for a photo.*

conceited *adj.* having too high an opinion of oneself. *My older sister is conceited about her looks.*
▷ **boastful** inclined to boast; bragging. *Alan is boastful about his good grades.*
▷ **vain** too proud of one's looks or accomplishments. *The queen was very vain and always admiring herself in the mirror.*

cook *v.* to prepare food for eating, using heat. *Dad will cook dinner.*

© McGraw-Hill School Division

▷ **bake** to cook in an oven. *Alice put the cake in the oven to bake.*

▷ **broil** to cook by exposing to a flame or another source of heat. *Let's broil the hamburgers on the grill.*

▷ **roast** cook with little moisture in the oven or over a fire. *Roast the turkey for six hours.*

cover See also **hide**.

cry *v.* to shed tears. *Julian wasn't sure what to do when he heard the baby cry.*

▷ **sob** to cry with short gasps. *Tina sobbed as she told us what happened.*

▷ **weep** to show grief, joy, or other strong emotions by crying. *James is happy—he will weep no more.*
ANTONYMS: See also **laugh**.

cure *v.* to bring back to health. *Rest will help cure that strained back.*

▷ **heal** to make better. *A doctor's job is to heal the sick.*

▷ **treat** to take care of an illness or injury. *A doctor should treat a high fever.*
ANTONYMS: make ill, harm, hurt, injure, poison

curious *adj.* eager to learn about something. *I am curious about new inventions.*

▷ **interested** wanting to find out about something. *Miguel is interested in the habits of whales.*

▷ **prying** looking or inquiring too closely. *I have been told that prying into someone's personal life can be impolite.*

D

danger *n.* a chance of harm or injury. *Fire is a danger to forests.*

▷ **hazard** something that can cause injury. *Bad weather can be a traffic hazard.*

▷ **menace** a person or thing that is a threat. *Careless drivers are a menace.*

▷ **risk** a chance of loss or harm. *Firefighters often place their lives at risk.*
ANTONYMS: safety

dark *adj.* having little or no light. *With no moon, it was a dark night.*

▷ **dim** having or giving little light; not bright. *There was only a dim light in the hall.*

▷ **shady** darker than the surrounding area. *We sat in a shady part of the yard.*

delicious *adj.* pleasing to the taste or smell. *The spaghetti sauce smelled delicious.*

▷ **flavorful** tasting good; full of flavor. *The apple was juicy and flavorful.*

depend *v.* to count on. *I can depend on my sister.*

▷ **rely** to trust in. *I will rely on you to be on time.*

▷ **trust** to have confidence in. *You can trust me to walk the dog twice a day.*
ANTONYMS: distrust, doubt

© McGraw-Hill School Division

disappear *v.* to go out of sight. *The jet will soon disappear into the clouds.*

▷ **evaporate** to fade away or end. *Your home run caused the other team's hopes for a win to evaporate.*

▷ **fade** to become fainter and disappear. *We heard the fire engines' sirens fade into the distance.*

▷ **vanish** to go out of sight or existence. *When you use this cleaner, stains will vanish.*

ANTONYMS: appear, reappear, remain

dislike *v.* to have a feeling of not liking. *I dislike okra.*

▷ **hate** to have very strong feelings against; dislike very much. *I hate losing a game!*

dive *v.* plunge headfirst. *It is not safe to dive here.*

▷ **plunge** to put in suddenly *I plunged my hand into the fish tank.*

do *v.* to carry out. *Mrs. Riley will do the job right.*

▷ **execute** to complete; to put into effect. *The soldier executed the orders.*

▷ **perform** to carry out to completion. *The doctor performed the operation.*

dry *adj.* not wet; free of moisture. *Please bring me a dry towel.*

▷ **arid** dry as a result of having little rainfall. *The Gobi desert is arid.*

▷ **parched** dried out by heat. *It was so hot, my throat was parched.*

ANTONYMS: See also **wet**.

easy *adj.* requiring little mental or physical effort; not difficult. *It is easy to count to ten.*

▷ **facile** not hard to do or achieve. *There is no facile solution to the problem of world hunger.*

▷ **simple** not complicated. *The directions for building the birdhouse were simple.*

ANTONYMS: hard, difficult

employ *v.* to pay someone to do a job. *Our neighbor will employ Rita to rake the leaves.*

▷ **appoint** to name for a job or an office. *The President can appoint certain judges.*

▷ **engage** to hire. *I will engage a secretary to take notes.*

▷ **hire** to give a job to. *If you hire me, I'll do a good job.*

ANTONYMS: fire, dismiss, let go, discharge

empty *adj.* having nothing or no one in it. *Mom washed out the empty vase.*

▷ **blank** not written or printed upon; unmarked. *One side of the paper was blank.*

▷ **vacant** containing no one or nothing; empty. *The parking lot is vacant.*

▷ **hollow** having an empty space inside. *The raccoons nested in a hollow log.*

enjoyment *n.* a happy or pleased feeling. *Baseball gives me much enjoyment.*

© McGraw-Hill School Division

▷ **delight** joy. *It is a delight to listen to good music.*

▷ **happiness** gladness. *Matthew got much happiness from the surprise party.*

▷ **pleasure** a satisfied or pleased feeling. *Pleasure can come from a job well done.*
ANTONYMS: dissatisfaction, unhappiness

equal *adj.* the same in size, amount, or value. *Five pennies are equal to one nickel.*

▷ **even** the same. *At the end of the fifth inning, the score in the game was even.*

▷ **matching** the same or similar, for example in size, color, or shape. *The sisters wore matching hats.*

▷ **similar** almost the same. *The two cars are similar but not exactly alike.*
ANTONYMS: unequal, different

F

fake *adj.* not real or genuine. *Billy wore a fake mustache.*

▷ **counterfeit** a copy made to cheat or fool someone. *The ten-dollar bill was counterfeit.*

▷ **false** not real; artificial *The actor wore a false nose.*

▷ **imitation** made to look like something real; artificial. *She had imitation roses on her hat.*
ANTONYMS: genuine, real

familiar *adj.* often heard or seen. *Seagulls are a familiar sight at the shore.*

▷ **common** happening often; usual. *Thunderstorms are common in summer.*

▷ **popular** liked or accepted by many people. *This restaurant is very popular.*

▷ **well-known** generally or widely known. *She is a well-known actress.*
ANTONYM: strange

far *adj.* a long way off; not near. *Steve's house is far from here.*

▷ **distant** extremely far. *Pluto is a distant planet.*

▷ **remote** faraway, in an out-of-the-way place. *We visited a remote village in the jungle.*
ANTONYMS: near, close

fast *adj.* moving or done with speed. *We rode on a fast train.*

▷ **quick** done in a very short time. *That was a quick game.*

▷ **rapid** with great speed, often in a continuing way. *Jeff kept walking at a rapid pace.*

▷ **swift** moving at great speed, often said of animals or people. *The swift runner flew by us.*
ANTONYM: slow

fear *n.* a feeling that trouble or danger is near. *He has a fear of heights.*

▷ **fright** a sudden, strong feeling of danger. *Surprising me like that gave me a real fright.*

© McGraw-Hill School Division

▷ **scare** a sudden panic. *We jumped out and gave them a scare.*

▷ **terror** a great feeling of danger. *The terror in the movie was caused by dinosaurs.*

ANTONYMS: fearlessness, courage, bravery

fine See also **good**.

friend *n.* a person one knows well and likes. *Kareem is my best friend.*

▷ **buddy** a close friend. *Warren has been my buddy since first grade.*

▷ **companion** a person or animal who often goes along with another person. *My dog is my constant companion.*

▷ **pal** a close friend. *My pal Theo and I play every day after school.*

ANTONYM: enemy

frown *v.* to express anger or sadness with a look on the face. *Mom will frown when she sees the mess our dog made.*

▷ **glare** to give an angry look. *A messy room will make him glare in anger.*

▷ **scowl** to look at in a displeased way. *The barking dog caused Lucy to scowl.*

ANTONYMS: smile, laugh, grin

funny *adj.* causing laughter. *Delia told us a funny joke.*

▷ **amusing** causing smiles of enjoyment or laughter. *That story was amusing.*

▷ *comical* causing laughter through actions. *The clowns were comical.*

▷ **entertaining** interesting; amusing. *We thought the movie was entertaining.*

▷ **hilarious** very funny and usually noisy. *That movie was hilarious.*

G

gentle *adj.* mild and kind; not rough. *Babies need gentle handling.*

▷ **soft** smooth to the touch; not hard or rough. *A soft breeze is blowing across the field.*

▷ **tender** delicate; kind and loving. *When I am sick, I need tender care.*

ANTONYMS: harsh, hard, rough

get *v.* to go for and return with. *Please get me a sandwich.*

▷ **acquire** to come into possession of through effort. *He acquired a new house.*

▷ **obtain** to get as one's own, often with some difficulty. *Lily worked hard to obtain her job.*

give *v.* to turn over possession or control of, to make a present of. *I am going to give my mother flowers for her birthday.*

▷ **confer** to give as an honor. *The college will confer a degree upon the guest speaker.*

▷ **contribute** to give in common with others. *We are asking each class to contribute a book to the library.*

© McGraw-Hill School Division

▷ **grant** to give in response to a request. *Grant me this favor.*

▷ **present** to give in a formal way. *Mr. Hammond will present the class gift.*

ANTONYMS: See also **take**.

go *v.* to move from one place to another. *We want to go to Florida for vacation.*

▷ **operate** to work. *This lawn mower won't operate without gas.*

▷ **run** to go quickly. *I have to run to the store to get more milk.*

▷ **travel** to make a trip. *Jessie wants to travel to France.*

▷ **wander** to move about with no particular place to go. *I like to wander through a bookstore and browse.*

ANTONYM: stay

good *adj.* Above average in quality. *This is a good book.*

▷ **excellent** extremely good. *Marie always does excellent work.*

▷ **expert** having a great deal of skill or knowledge. *The gardener gave us expert advice on planting the tree.*

▷ **fair** somewhat good; slightly better than average. *Jeremy did a fair job.*

▷ **fine** of high quality; very good. *She made a fine dinner for the party.*

▷ **terrific** extremely good; wonderful. *Juanita had a terrific idea.*

▷ **wonderful** very good; excellent. *I had a wonderful time at the party.*

ANTONYMS: bad, poor

graceful *adj.* pleasing in design or movement. *The dancer's movements were graceful.*

▷ **agile** able to move quickly and easily. *The agile skater made the turns look easy.*

▷ **nimble** light and quick in movement. *The gymnast was nimble as she did her routine.*

▷ **quick** reacting easily and rapidly. *With one quick movement, the cat leaped onto the fence.*

▷ **smooth** able, skillful in movement. *The skater's smooth turns and jumps were awesome to watch.*

ANTONYMS: awkward, clumsy

great *adj.* of unusual quality or ability. *Mark Twain was a great writer.*

▷ **huge** very big; enormous. *The play was a huge success.*

▷ **important** having great value or meaning. *Marie Curie made an important contribution to science.*

▷ **remarkable** having unusual qualities. *That was a remarkable movie.*

▷ **superb** of greater quality than most. *She is a superb singer.*

See also **good**.

© McGraw-Hill School Division

guess *v.* to form an opinion without enough information. *I guess there are six hundred marbles in that jar.*
▷ **estimate** to form an opinion of the value or cost of something. *I estimate that it will cost $50.00 to repair the bike.*
▷ **suppose** to believe that something is possible but not certain. *I suppose Jean will lend you her scarf.*

H

halfway *adv.* to or at half the distance. *Tad fell halfway through the race.*
▷ **midway** in the middle; halfway. *Your house is midway between Sam's and mine.*

happy *adj.* having, showing, or bringing pleasure. *Mr. Andersen was happy in his garden.*
▷ **cheerful** showing or feeling cheer or happiness. *The cheerful boy whistled as he worked.*
▷ **glad** feeling or expressing joy or pleasure. *Tony was glad to visit the museum.*
▷ **joyful** very happy; filled with joy. *A wedding is a joyful occasion.*
▷ **merry** happy and cheerful. *The party was a merry occasion.*
▷ **pleased** satisfied or content. *Harry was pleased with the new coat.*
ANTONYMS: See also **sad**.

hard *adj.* not easy to do or deal with. *Mowing the lawn is hard work.*
▷ **difficult** hard to do; requiring effort. *Steering a ship through a storm is a difficult task.*
▷ *tough* difficult to do, often in a physical sense. *Catching wild horses is a tough job.*
ANTONYM: easy

harm *v.* to cause someone or something injury or problems. *You can harm a plant by not giving it water.*
▷ **damage** to harm or make less valuable. *Carelessness can cause damage to property.*
▷ *hurt* to give pain to. *If you fight, you will hurt each other.*
▷ **injure** to hurt. *Rose wears a helmet, so she will not injure herself when she rides her bike.*
ANTONYMS: help, aid, protect, heal

help *v.* to provide with support; to be of service to. *Will you help me clean this floor?*
▷ **aid** to give help to someone in trouble. *The police aided us in finding the lost children.*
▷ **assist** to help, often in a cooperative way. *Ned assisted his brother in painting the house.*

hide *v.* to put or keep out of sight. *The bird will hide its eggs.*
▷ **cover** to hide. *The blowing snow soon covered his tracks.*
▷ **conceal** to put or keep out of sight. *The thick shrubs conceal the groundhog's hole.*

© McGraw-Hill School Division

high *adj.* located or extending a great distance above the ground. *The bird soared high above the treetops.*

▷ **tall** having a height greater than average but with a relatively narrow width. *Over the years, the pine trees grew to be very tall.*

▷ **towering** of great or imposing height. *The towering buildings shadowed the people below.*
ANTONYMS: low, short

hot *adj.* having a high temperature; having much heat. *The oven is hot.*

▷ **fiery** as hot as fire; burning. *The spaceship flew toward the fiery sun.*

▷ **scalding** hot enough to burn, often said of liquids. *A pot of scalding water fell on the floor.*

▷ **scorching** hot enough to cause burning or drying. *The scorching sun blazed down on the weary travelers.*
ANTONYMS: See also **cold**.

house *n.* a building in which people live. *Franz lives in the white house on the corner.*

▷ **cabin** a small simple house often built of logs or boards. *Lincoln was born in a log cabin.*

▷ **home** a place where a person lives. *Our home is in an apartment building.*

hurt *v.* to cause pain or damage. *Did you hurt your knee?*

▷ **harm** to do damage to. *A good rider would never harm a horse.*

▷ **injure** to cause physical damage. *Jon fell and injured his leg.*

I

idea *n.* a picture or thought formed in the mind. *Pedro had an idea for a new invention.*

▷ **inspiration** a sudden, bright idea. *Using the old skateboard to make a wagon was pure inspiration.*

▷ **opinion** a belief based on what a person thinks and that cannot be proven true or untrue. *In my opinion, chocolate tastes better than vanilla.*

▷ **thought** a product of thinking; an idea or opinion. *What are your thoughts on this problem?*

important adj. having great value or meaning. Education is very important.

▷ **major** chief or most important. *The major reason I jog is to relax.*

▷ **significant** having special value or meaning. *July 4th is a significant day in American history.*

interesting *adj.* arousing or holding interest or attention. *That was an interesting book.*

▷ **captivating** capturing and holding the attention by beauty or excellence. *Grandpa told us a captivating story about life long ago.*

▷ **fascinating** causing and holding the interest through a special quality or charm. *The snake charmer's act was fascinating.*
ANTONYMS: dull, boring

© McGraw-Hill School Division

J

job *n.* position of work or piece of work to be done. *It is my job to feed the dog.*

▷ **employment** the work a person does. *He found employment in a shoe factory.*

▷ **assignment** something that is given out as a task. *We worked on our history assignment.*

▷ **duty** something someone is supposed to do. *It is a host's duty to make guests feel welcome.*

▷ **occupation** the work a person does to earn a living. *My uncle's occupation was photography.*

▷ **profession** an occupation that requires special education and training. *Sarah wants to make medicine her profession.*

journey *n.* a long trip. *The journey to North America was full of hardships.*

▷ **expedition** a journey made for a particular reason. *Peary and Henson made several expeditions to reach the North Pole.*

▷ **trip** the act of going from one place to another. *We made the trip to Chicago by plane.*

junk *n.* old things that are no longer useful. *We cleaned the junk out of the garage.*

▷ **rubbish** trash *We put the rubbish in the alley.*

▷ **trash** unwanted things to be thrown away. *Should I put this broken toy in the trash?*

▷ **scrap** worn or used material that can be used again. *We saved the scrap wood for kindling.*

K

know *v.* to understand clearly; be certain of the facts or truth of. *I know where he lives.*

▷ **realize** to understand completely. *I didn't realize you wanted to come with us.*

▷ **recognize** to know and remember from before. *Did you recognize your former teacher when you met her at the mall?*

▷ **understand** to get the meaning of; comprehend. *I finally understand why you've been having trouble!*

L

large See also **big**.

lazy *adj.* not willing to work. *My dog is too lazy to chase cats.*

▷ **idle** not active *We spent an idle afternoon resting in the shade.*

▷ **inactive** not lively or busy. *Even though Joe's grandfather retired, he's is not inactive.*
ANTONYMS: active, busy

laugh *v.* to make the sounds and facial movements that show amusement. *He laughs at my jokes.*

▷ **chuckle** to laugh softly, especially to oneself. *Carla chuckled when she read my note.*

© McGraw-Hill School Division

▷ **giggle** to laugh in a silly, high-pitched, or nervous way. *Jill giggled and turned red.*

▷ **guffaw** to laugh loudly. *Henry guffawed so hard, he had to hold his sides.*

ANTONYMS: See also **cry**.

let *v.* to give permission to. *Mom won't let me go to the game.*

▷ **allow** to grant permission to or for, usually in relation to rules. *The rules do not allow fishing on the beach.*

▷ **permit** to allow (a person) to do something. *He will permit you to use the pool if you ask.*

ANTONYMS: deny, refuse, forbid

like *v.* to take pleasure in (something); to feel affection for (someone). *I like to go walking in the rain.*

▷ **admire** to have affection and respect for (someone). *Johnny admires his grandfather.*

▷ **enjoy** to take pleasure in (something). *Shelley enjoys music.*

▷ **love** to like (something) a lot; to feel great affection for (someone). *Mary loves to go sailing.*

ANTONYMS: dislike, hate

listen *v.* to try to hear; pay attention. *Listen when the teacher is speaking.*

▷ **hear** to receive sound through the ears. *Do you hear what I'm saying?*

▷ **heed** to pay careful attention to; listen or mind. *I will heed my parents' advice and wear a sweater to the ball game.*

ANTONYMS: ignore

little *adj.* small in size; not big. little *adj.* small in size. *A pebble is a little stone.*

▷ **short** not long or tall. *My legs are too short to reach the floor from this chair.*

▷ **slight** not much or not important. *Our chances of winning are slight.*

▷ **small** not large *A mouse is a small animal.*

▷ **tiny** very small. *The baby has tiny fingers.*

ANTONYMS: See also **big**.

look *v.* to see with one's eyes. *She looked at the moon.*

▷ **glance** to look quickly. *Kenny only glanced at the book.*

▷ **peer** to look closely. *Moe peered at the map to find the town.*

▷ **stare** to look at for a long time with eyes wide open. *Sue was so surprised she just stared at me.* See also **see**.

loud *adj.* having a strong sound. *We heard a loud crash overhead.*

▷ **deafening** loud enough to make one deaf. *The dam broke with a deafening roar.*

▷ **noisy** full of sounds, often unpleasant. *The crowd was noisy.*

ANTONYMS: See also **quiet**.

loudly *adv.* in a loud way. *The doorbell rang loudly.*

▷ **noisily** in a loud, harsh way. *The children played noisily on the playground.*

© McGraw-Hill School Division

loyal *adj.* having or showing strong and lasting affection. *Sue is a loyal friend.*

▷ **faithful** loyal and devoted. *Lad was a faithful companion to his old master.*

▷ **true** faithful to someone or something. *A true friend is there when you need help.*

▷ **trustworthy** reliable; able to be trusted. *I only told my most trustworthy friends.*

love *v.* to have a strong, warm feeling for. *I love my pets very much.*

▷ **adore** to love greatly. *The children adore their aunt.*

▷ **enjoy** to get joy or pleasure from, be happy with. *I enjoy the company of my sisters.*
ANTONYMS: dislike, hate, loathe, despise

lying *v.* stretching out. *It is easier to fall asleep lying down than sitting up.*

▷ **reclining** leaning back, lying down. *Jake is reclining on the sofa and reading a book.*

▷ **sprawling** lying or sitting with the body stretched out in an awkward or careless manner. *My dog spent the morning sprawling on the rug with his eyes closed.*
ANTONYMS: standing, sitting

M

many *adj.* consisting of a large number. *Dave has many socks.*

▷ **countless** too many to be counted. *We picked countless raspberries to make jam.*

▷ **innumerable** too many to be numbered or counted. *Innumerable people lined the streets for the parade.*

▷ **numerous** a great many. *I have asked you numerous times.*

▷ **plenty** (of) enough, or more than enough, suggesting a large number. *We have plenty of plates.*

▷ **several** more than a few but fewer than many. *Keiko has played in several games this season.*
ANTONYM: few

mean *adj.* lacking in kindness or understanding. *Joe felt bad about being mean to his sister.*

▷ **cruel** willing to cause pain or suffering. *It is cruel to hurt an animal.*

▷ **nasty** resulting from hate. *That was a nasty trick he played on us.*

▷ **selfish** concerned only about oneself. *Kelley is too selfish to care about my feelings.*

▷ **spiteful** filled with ill feelings toward others. *Pat is a spiteful person.*
ANTONYMS: See also **nice**.

mild *adj.* not extreme. *Jackie likes food with a mild taste, but Jon prefers spicy dishes.*

▷ **bland** without any harsh or extreme qualities. *Rice and cottage cheese are bland foods.*

© McGraw-Hill School Division

▷ **calm** quiet. *The ocean is calm, and the wind is still.*

▷ **soothing** able to ease irritation. *The cream was soothing on his chapped skin.*

ANTONYMS: rough, wild, fierce, harsh, strong, extreme, spicy

N

neat *adj.* clean and orderly. *His clothes always look neat.*

▷ **tidy** neat and clean, often said of a place. *She likes to keep her room tidy.*

▷ **well-groomed** carefully dressed and groomed. *Marvin always looks well-groomed at school.*

ANTONYMS: messy, untidy, sloppy

new *adj.* having just come into being, use, or possession. *I need to sharpen this new pencil.*

▷ **different** not alike or similar. *Tim's solution to the problem was different from anyone else's.*

▷ **fresh** seeming new and unaffected by time. *We put fresh flowers in the vase.*

▷ **modern** having to do with the present time; up-to-date. *Modern computers are different from ones used 30 years ago.*

▷ **original** not thought of or heard before. *Amanda had an original idea for a class play.*

▷ **recent** referring to a time just before the present. *Their recent victory made the team confident.*

▷ **unfamiliar** not known before; strange. *Aunt Sarah took us to lunch in an unfamiliar part of town.*

▷ **young** in the early part of life. *Pal is still a young dog.*

ANTONYMS: old; old-fashioned

nice *adj.* agreeable or pleasing. *Lynn is a nice person.*

▷ **gentle** mild and kindly in manner. *He is so gentle with the children.*

▷ **kind** gentle and friendly; good-hearted. *Uncle Bob was very kind to send you a gift.*

▷ **pleasant** agreeable; giving pleasure to. *She has a pleasant way of talking.*

▷ **sweet** having or marked by agreeable or pleasing qualities. *He wrote a sweet thank-you note.*

ANTONYMS: See also **mean**.

noise *n.* any sound, but especially one that is loud or harsh. *The traffic noise gives me a headache.*

▷ **commotion** noisy confusion; disorder. *The runaway goat caused a commotion in the supermarket.*

▷ **din** a loud noise that continues for some time. *I couldn't hear him over the din of the traffic.*

▷ **racket** loud or confusing noise. *There was such a racket in the restaurant that we couldn't have a conversation.*

nothing *n.* not anything. *Ten minus ten leaves nothing.*

▷ **none** no one or not one. *Six people started the problem, but none solved it.*

© McGraw-Hill School Division

▷ **zero** nothing. *If none of your answers on the test are correct, your score will be zero.*
ANTONYMS: something, anything, everything, all

O

offer *v.* to present for acceptance or rejection. *If you are hungry, I can offer you a peanut butter sandwich.*
▷ **propose** to put forward a plan. We propose to write an outline before we do the report.
▷ **suggest** to mention as a possibility. I suggest that we leave for home before it gets dark.

often *adv.* many times; again and again. *Theo often visits his sister.*
▷ **frequently** happening again and again. *Sarah frequently works late.*
▷ **regularly** happening at fixed times. *Mrs. Day regularly takes the bus.*
ANTONYMS: seldom, rarely

old *adj.* having lived or existed for a long time. *My grandmother's favorite vase is very old.*
▷ **aged** having grown old. *Minnie helps take care of her aged aunt.*
▷ **ancient** of great age; very old; of times long past. *Dr. Tyrell found an ancient coin.*
▷ **elderly** rather old. *Our elderly neighbor swims every day.*
ANTONYM: young. See also **new**.

open *adj.* not having its lid, door, or other covering closed. *It was easy to see the toys in the open toy chest.*
▷ **unclosed** not having its door or other covering shut. *An unclosed box will allow dust to get inside.*
▷ **uncovered** not having the lid or cover on. *Steam rose from the uncovered soup pot cooking on the stove.*
ANTONYMS: closed, shut, covered, locked

P

peace *n.* quiet; calm. *Mom asked for ten minutes of peace and quiet.*
▷ **calm** a time of quiet or stillness. *A great calm settled over us.*
▷ **stillness** absence of noise or motion. *In the stillness, the only thing I heard was my own breathing.*
▷ **tranquillity** freedom from noise or disturbance. *We enjoy the tranquillity of this hidden pond.*
▷ **quiet** the condition of little noise or disturbance. *I like to read in the quiet of my own room.*
ANTONYMS: confusion, commotion

perfect *adj.* without flaw or error in its appearance or nature. *A perfect math test is one with no mistakes.*
▷ **faultless** without error—often describing performance or behavior. *The gymnast performed a faultless routine.*

© McGraw-Hill School Division

▷ **flawless** without imperfections such as marks or bumps. *The marble's smooth surface was flawless.*

▷ **ideal** exactly what is hoped for or needed. *Blue is the ideal color for these walls.*
ANTONYMS: imperfect, faulty, flawed, marred

plain *adj.* not distinguished from others in any way. *The villagers are plain, hard-working people.*

▷ **common** average; not special. *He lives like any common person.*

▷ **ordinary** plain; average; everyday. *It's just an ordinary newspaper.*
ANTONYM: special. See also **unusual**.

pretty *adj.* pleasing or attractive to the senses. *That is a pretty flower.*

▷ **attractive** having an appealing quality; pleasing. *She is tall and attractive.*

▷ **beautiful** having pleasant qualities. *That is the most beautiful movie I saw this year.*

▷ **gorgeous** extremely beautiful or richly colored. *The fireworks display was gorgeous.*
ANTONYMS: ugly, hideous, unattractive. See also **plain**.

problem *n.* a question to be thought about and answered. *We tried to think of solutions to our problem.*

▷ **maze** a confusing series of paths or passageways. *The shrubs formed a maze in the garden.*

▷ **tangle** a twisted confused mass. *The situation was caused by a tangle of misunderstandings.*

▷ **riddle** a question or problem that is hard to understand. *The solution to the mystery was in the form of a riddle.*

proud *adj.* having a sense of one's own worth, usually in a positive way. *He was proud of his new baby sister.*

▷ **conceited** having too high an opinion of oneself, in a negative way. *Shelley is too conceited to talk to me.*

▷ **haughty** having or showing much pride in oneself. *He is a haughty football hero.*

▷ **pleased** having given pleasure to, or received pleasure from. *I was pleased that he wanted to come with us.*
ANTONYMS: humble

Q

question *n.* a matter to be talked over. *We discussed the question of sports clubs.*

▷ **issue** a matter to be thought about, not necessarily a problem. *Recycling is an issue that many people have opinions about.*

▷ **problem** a matter needing to be solved. *The meeting will deal with the problem of noise.*

▷ **topic** a subject or matter to be examined. *What is the topic of your speech?*

© McGraw-Hill School Division

quick *adj.* done in a short time; fast. *We had a quick lunch at the diner.*
▷ **fast** acting, moving, or done in a short time. *This is a fast car.*
▷ **rapid** very quick; fast *We had a rapid trip on the train.*
▷ **swift** able to move very quickly. *The cheetah is a swift runner.*
ANTONYM: slow

quick *adv.* thinking, learning, or reacting easily or rapidly. *Jane's quick mind solved the problem easily.*
▷ **clever** having a quick mind; bright and alert. *John is clever at crossword puzzles.*
▷ **keen** sharp or quick in seeing, hearing, or thinking. *The fox has keen hearing.*
▷ **intelligent** having or showing the ability to think, learn and understand. *Do scientists think dolphins are intelligent?*

quiet *adj.* with little or no noise. *The house was quiet after everyone had gone.*
▷ **calm** free of excitement or strong feeling; quiet. *Remember to be calm during an emergency.*
▷ **humble** modest; not proud or showy. *Joe helps others in a humble way.*
▷ **peaceful** calm; undisturbed. *The camp is so peaceful early in the morning.*
▷ **silent** completely quiet; without noise. *The band members were silent until the leader raised the baton.*
▷ **still** without sound; silent. *The forest was still.*
▷ **wordless** without using words to communicate. *With a wordless gesture, Michelle told us to come quickly.*
ANTONYMS: loud, noisy

R

reach *v.* to come to. *We will reach the hotel by sunset.*
▷ **approach** to come near. *The ships slow down as they approach the dock.*
▷ **arrive** to get to or come to. *When you arrive at the museum, wait for me in the front hall.*
▷ **land** to come to the ground or to shore. *The plane should land at the airport soon.*
ANTONYMS: leave, go, depart

ready *adj.* fit for use or action. *Everything is ready for the party.*
▷ **prepared** ready or fit for a particular purpose. *Jim was prepared for the test.*
▷ **set** ready or prepared to do something. *Willie was all set to go to school.*

really *adv.* in fact. *What really happened at the store today?*
▷ **actually** in fact; really. *Dan actually got his first job yesterday!*
▷ **indeed** really; truly. *I was indeed waiting for you at the park.*
▷ **truly** in fact; really. *He truly did earn ten dollars.*

© McGraw-Hill School Division

right *adj.* free from error; true. *Every single answer was right.*

▷ **accurate** without errors. *His description was accurate.*

▷ **correct** agreeing with fact or truth. *He found the correct way to solve the puzzle.*

▷ *exact* very accurate; completely correct. *Each math problem has an exact answer.*

ANTONYMS: wrong, mistaken

roar *v.* to speak or make sounds in a loud, deep voice. *If she hits a home run, the crowd will roar.*

▷ **bellow** to make a loud sound or speak very loudly. *Why does he bellow if I'm standing right here?*

▷ **scream** to make a sudden, sharp, loud cry. *This fake spider made my brother scream.*

▷ **shout** to call loudly. *The announcer had to shout to be heard over the cheering audience.*

▷ **yell** to give a loud cry, or to speak loudly. *I heard him yell, "We won!"*

rude *adj.* not polite; ill-mannered. *Jack made a rude remark.*

▷ **discourteous** without good manners. *You have no reason to be discourteous to Mr. Braun.*

▷ **impolite** not showing good manners. *They were impolite when they left the party without saying "good-bye."*

ANTONYMS: polite, courteous

run *v.* to go quickly on foot. *I can run much faster now than I did last year.*

▷ **dash** to go very fast; to run with sudden speed. *Lou dashed to the door when the mailman came with his birthday cards.*

▷ **race** to run very fast; to run in competition with. *The girls raced the boys in the class Olympics.*

▷ **scurry** to move hurriedly. *The puppies scurried to their food dish.*

S

sad *adj.* feeling or showing unhappiness or sorrow. *Jake was sad when he lost his dog.*

▷ **depressed** feeling low; sad. *We were depressed when we could not find our dog.*

▷ **downcast** low in spirits; sad. *She was downcast when she did not make the team.*

▷ **miserable** extremely unhappy. *Mary was miserable after her brother left for college.*

ANTONYMS: See also **happy**.

same *adj.* being just like something else in kind, quantity, or degree. *Both pieces of cake are the same size.*

▷ **alike** similar, showing a resemblance. *The twin sisters look alike.*

▷ **equal** the same in size, amount, quality, or value. *Four and four equals six and two.*

© McGraw-Hill School Division

▷ **identical** the same in every detail. *Our house is identical to the one around the block.* ANTONYM: different

say *v.* to make known or express in words. *Mel says that he wants to go home.*

▷ **comment** to make a remark or give an opinion. *Our teacher commented about our oral reports.*

▷ **exclaim** to express surprise or other strong feeling. *"You wouldn't really go there,!" exclaimed Bill.*

▷ **declare** to make known publicly or formally. *The mayor declared that the town needed more money.*

▷ **pronounce** to say formally or officially that something is so. *The minister pronounced the couple married.*

▷ **speak** to express an idea, or a feeling. *Wendy spoke to us about the new park.*

▷ **state** to express or explain fully in words. *Mr. Combs stated his opinion during the meeting.*

▷ **talk** to express ideas or information; to speak. *Ken talked about his model airplane.* See also **tell**.

scared *adj.* afraid; alarmed. *Sheila was scared when she heard a noise.*

▷ **afraid** feeling fear, often in a continuing way or for a long time. *Jerry is afraid of the dark.*

▷ **fearful** filled with fear. *Donna was fearful of the thunder.*

▷ **frightened** scared suddenly or for a short time. *He was frightened when the lights went out.*

▷ **terrified** extremely scared; filled with terror. *Pete was terrified when he heard the screams.*

search *v.* to look, look through, or examine carefully in order to find something. *Please help me search for my mittens!*

▷ **discover** to see or find out for the first time. *Did Irish monks discover North America before the Vikings?*

▷ **explore** to go to a place that one knows nothing about. *Let's explore the woods behind the new mall.*

▷ **seek** to try to find, go in search of. *The Keeper of the Gate asked, "Whom do you seek?"*

see *v.* to receive impressions through the use of the eyes. *She could see the children playing across the street.*

▷ **observe** to notice. *What did you observe during the science experiment?*

▷ **view** to look at, usually for a purpose. *Many people wanted to view the sculpture.* See also **look**.

sensible *adj.* having or showing good sense; wise. *It is sensible to wear a helmet when riding a bike.*

▷ **logical** having to do with sound reasoning. *Taking the train was the logical choice.*

© McGraw-Hill School Division

▷ **reasonable** showing or using good sense; not foolish. *We gave him a reasonable amount of time to finish the project.*

▷ **wise** having or showing good judgment or intelligence. *Jill knows it is wise not to touch strange dogs.*
ANTONYMS: foolish, silly

show *v.* to bring to sight. *Please show me your collection.*

▷ **display** to show or exhibit. *Joey likes to display his model car collection.*

▷ **prove** to show that something is as it is supposed to be. *You can prove that blue and yellow make green.*

▷ **produce** to bring forth; show. *The judge told the lawyer to produce his evidence at the trial.*

▷ **reveal** to make known. *The magician refused to reveal his secret.*

shy *adj.* uncomfortable in the presence of others. *Paula is too shy to speak in front of the class.*

▷ **bashful** easily embarrassed; very shy. *Carl was too bashful to step out from behind the chair.*

▷ **timid** showing a lack of courage; easily frightened. *The timid little boy would not go near the cows.*
ANTONYM: bold

sick adj. having poor health. Ted was sick in bed all last week.

▷ **ill** not healthy; sick. *Mark stayed home from school because he was ill.*

▷ **unwell** not feeling well. *Stan has felt unwell for a month.*
ANTONYMS: well, healthy

small See also **little**.

smart *adj.* intelligent; bright; having learned much. *Tommy is a smart boy for his age.*

▷ **clever** mentally sharp; quick-witted. *Some people think that foxes are clever.*

▷ **intelligent** able to learn, understand, and reason. *Shana is an intelligent girl.*

▷ **wise** able to know or judge what is right, good, or true, often describing a person with good sense rather than one who knows a lot of facts. *The chief was a wise old man.*
ANTONYM: stupid

smile *v.* to show a smile, in a happy or friendly way. *May Li smiled when she saw the puppy.*

▷ **grin** to smile broadly with real happiness or amusement. *Keith grinned when he saw my costume.*

▷ **smirk** to smile in a silly or self-satisfied way. *Pat smirked at him because she knew the answer.*
ANTONYMS: frown, scowl

stay *v.* to wait in one place; remain. *I will stay here and wait.*

▷ **remain** stay behind or in the same place. *You go ahead; I'll remain here.*

▷ **visit** stay with as a guest. *My aunt plans to visit us next month.*

© McGraw-Hill School Division

strange *adj.* differing from the usual or the ordinary. *That is a strange little dog.*
  ▷ **odd** not ordinary. *She has some very odd clothes.*
  ▷ **weird** strange or odd, in a frightening or mysterious way. *Kids say the weird house is haunted.*
  See also **unusual**.

strong *adj.* having great strength or physical power. *Football players have to be strong.*
  ▷ **mighty** having great power. *Paul Bunyan was a mighty man.*
  ▷ **muscular** having well-developed muscles; strong. *Lifting weights has made Neil muscular.*
  ▷ **powerful** having great strength, influence, or authority. *The governor is a powerful woman.*
  ANTONYM: weak

sudden *adj.* happening quickly and without warning. *The sudden bang from the car's engine made me jump.*
  ▷ **quick** fast. *The quick movement of the cat's paw surprised the squirrel.*
  ▷ **startling** surprising; happening without warning. *The outcome of the elections was startling to all of us.*
  ▷ **unexpected** coming without warning, but not necessarily sudden. *An unexpected storm flooded the streets.*
  ▷ **unpredicted** not guessed or expected ahead of time. *The team's win had unpredicted results.*

sure *adj.* firmly believing in something. *Pam is sure that our team will win.*
  ▷ **certain** free from doubt; very sure. *Russ is certain of his answer.*
  ▷ **confident** firmly trusting; sure of oneself or of another. *Mac is confident that he will get the job.*
  ▷ **definite** positive or certain. *It is definite that school is closed on Friday.*
  ANTONYMS: doubtful, unsure

surprised *adj.* feeling sudden wonder. *Joan was surprised when she heard she had won the award.*
  ▷ **amazed** overwhelmed with wonder or surprise. *I was amazed when the dog did as I asked.*
  ▷ **astonished** greatly surprised; shocked. *Everyone was astonished when snow fell in June.*
  ▷ **astounded** greatly surprised; stunned. *Lynn was so astounded that she could not move.*

T

take *v.* to get into one's hands or possession; to obtain. *May I take your tray for you?*
  ▷ **grab** to take roughly or rudely. *Brianne grabbed the paper and wrote a quick note.*
  ▷ **seize** to take suddenly and by force. *The policemen seized the runaway prisoner.*

© McGraw-Hill School Division

▷ **snatch** to take suddenly and quickly, often in secret. *The dog snatched a bone off the table when no one was looking.*
ANTONYMS: See **give**.

talk See **say**.

tame *adj.* not fearful or shy; not wild. *I tried to tame the chipmunk.*
▷ **gentle** easy to handle; tame. *Darcy chose a gentle horse for me to ride.*
▷ **obedient** tending or willing to obey. *Champ is an obedient dog.*
ANTONYMS: wild, fierce, unruly

tell *v.* to put or express in written or spoken words. *Mandy told us about camp.*
▷ **announce** to state or make known publicly. *Mrs. Grimes announced that she would be leaving.*
▷ **narrate** to tell about events, especially a story. *The camp leader narrated a spooky story.*
▷ **relate** to tell or report events or details. *Paul related the story of how we got lost in the woods.*
See also **say**.

thick *adj.* having much space from one side to the other; not thin
▷ **bulky** large in size. *This package is too bulky to fit easily into the car.*
▷ **dense** growing close together. *We could hardly get through the dense underbrush.*
ANTONYM: thin, sparse

thin *adj.* not fat. *His father has always been rather thin.*
▷ **lean** with little or no fat but often strong. *A runner must have a lean body.*
▷ **skinny** very thin in an unhealthy way. *Joe was very skinny when he was sick.*
▷ **slender** thin in a pleasing way. *The model was tall and slender.*
▷ **slim** thin, in a good or healthy way. *Dennis has gotten slim since he started exercising.*
ANTONYMS: fat, plump

think *v.* to have in mind as an opinion or attitude. *Kim thinks we should have a picnic.*
▷ **believe** to accept as true or real. *She believes my story.*
▷ **consider** to regard; to believe. *The coach considers Nick to be his best player.*

U

unusual *adj.* not usual, common, or ordinary. *Her eyes are an unusual color.*
▷ **different** not alike or similar. *The color we painted my bedroom is really different!*
▷ **extraordinary** very unusual; beyond the ordinary. *That painting is an extraordinary piece of art.*
▷ **peculiar** not usual, strange; queer. *While we were sitting by the campfire, we heard a peculiar noise from the woods.*

© McGraw-Hill School Division

▷ **rare** seldom happening, seen, or found. *Bald eagles are rare birds.*
▷ **uncommon** rare or unusual. *Hurricanes are uncommon in this area.*
See also **strange**.
ANTONYMS: common, usual

upset *adj.* feeling uneasy; distressed. *Tina was upset when no one came to her party.*
▷ **anxious** uneasy about or fearful of what may happen. *The first-graders were anxious on the first day of school.*
▷ **concerned** troubled or worried. *Mom was concerned when my brother was late.*
▷ **worried** uneasy or troubled about something. *Jack was worried that the river would flood.*
ANTONYM: calm

V

very *adv.* to a great extent. *The summer day was very hot.*
▷ **considerably** to a large or an important degree. *It will be considerably warmer tomorrow.*
▷ **extremely** greatly or intensely. *The sun overhead is extremely hot.*
▷ **somewhat** to some extent. *We were somewhat surprised by the news.*

W

walk *v.* to move or travel on foot. *Ruth walked across the street.*
▷ **march** to walk with regular steps. *The band marched down the street.*
▷ **shuffle** to drag the feet when walking. *The children shuffled through the dry leaves.*
▷ **stride** to walk with long steps, usually with a purpose. *We watched him stride down the hall.*
▷ **stroll** to walk in a relaxed, slow way. *Let's stroll around the mall.*
▷ **strut** to walk in a vain or very proud way. *Joe likes to strut up and down in his new clothes.*

want *v.* to have a desire or wish for. *Lenny wants lunch.*
▷ **crave** to want badly, often in an uncontrollable way. *Suzanne ran to the store because she craved ice cream.*
▷ **desire** to have a strong wish for. *Molly desired fame and fortune.*
▷ **long** to want very much. *I long to see my old friends again.*
▷ **require** to have a need of. *We all require food and sleep.*
▷ **wish** to have a longing or strong need for. *Gary wished he could have a horse in the city.*
▷ **yearn** to feel a strong and deep desire. *Grandpa yearned for the warm days of summer.*

© McGraw-Hill School Division

weak *adj.* not having strength, force, or power. *The light is too weak to read by.*

▷ **feeble** not strong; weak. *The sick puppy was too feeble to stand up.*

▷ **frail** lacking in strength; weak. *This chair is too frail to hold a person.*

▷ **powerless** without power; helpless. *The mouse was powerless in the cat's claws.*

ANTONYM: See also **strong**.

wet *adj.* covered or soaked with water or another liquid. *Her hair was wet after the long swim.*

▷ **damp** slightly wet. *Our bathing suits are still damp.*

▷ **moist** slightly wet; damp. *Use a moist cloth to wipe up the dust.*

▷ **sopping** extremely wet; dripping. *Lisa's clothes were sopping after being caught in the sudden storm.*

ANTONYMS: See also **dry**.

whole *adj.* made up of the entire amount, quantity, or number. *Did you eat that whole pizza?*

▷ **complete** having all its parts. *Is that a complete set of crayons?*

▷ **entire** whole; having all its parts. *The entire class had to stay after school.*

▷ **total** whole, full, or entire, often referring to numbers. *Did you pay the total amount?*

wide *adj.* covering a large area from side to side. *The doorway to the gym is very wide.*

▷ **broad** large from one side to the other side. *Jim had a broad grin when his bike won the prize.*

▷ **extensive** large; great; broad. *The hurricane caused extensive damage.*

ANTONYM: narrow

wild *adj.* not controlled by people; not tamed. *There are wild horse in the desert.*

▷ **fierce** dangerous; savage. *Any injured animal can be fierce.*

▷ **savage** not tamed; wild. *The animals in the zoo are still savage animals.*

McGraw-Hill Language Arts
Grade 4, Unit 6

90

© McGraw-Hill School Division

Vocabulary Strategies

How many thousands of words do you know? Your **vocabulary** is made up of all the words you know, including their definitions. With a great vocabulary you're able to communicate exactly what you mean. A good vocabulary will also help you inderstand what you read. Use these strategies to build your vocabulary.

Context Clues

Often you can figure out the meaning of an unfamiliar word by looking at the words around it — that is, the word's **context**.

Word Parts

Many words can be divided into a beginning, middle, and end. Knowing the meaning of its **word parts** can help you to figure out what a word means.

Homophones and Homographs

Homophones are words that sound the same but have different meanings and different spellings.

Homographs are words that have the same spelling but mean different things.

© McGraw-Hill School Division

Idioms

Idioms are sayings. They aren't supposed to be taken literally. Recognizing an idiom is the first step to figuring out what it means.

Etymology

Etymology means "the origins of a word." English is an amazing blend of words from other languages. Clues about a word's etymology can help you figure out its meaning.

A Dictionary

A **dictionary** is a reference book that lists words and gives their definitions.

A Thesaurus

A **thesaurus** is a reference book that lists synonyms. Any two words that have the same or similar meaning are synonyms. A thesaurus is a useful tool for finding just the right word for the meaning you are trying to express.

© McGraw-Hill School Division

The Elements of a Dictionary

Guide words   Are the first and last words on the page. They help you to find the word you're looking for.

Entry word   Shows how a word is spelled. If the word is longer than one syllable, it's divided into syllables; dots are placed between syllables.

Pronunciation guide   Shows how a word is pronounced. Use the **pronunciation key**—there's usually one inside the dictionary's front and back covers—to see the specific sounds of each letter.

Part-of-speech label   Shows how the word can be used in a sentence, such as **n.** for noun, **v.** for verb, or **adj.** for adjective. Sometimes a word can be used as more than one part of speech.

Definitions   Shows the various meanings of a word. If there are more than one, the definitions are numbered, with the most widely used meaning listed first.

Example sentences   Show how the word can be used in a sentence.

Inflected forms   Show the plural form of nouns, the past and present participles of verbs, and the comparative and superlative forms of adjectives.

Etymology   Gives the origin and history of the word.

© McGraw-Hill School Division

Pronunciation Key

Symbol	Sample Words		Symbol	Sample Words
a	at, bad		ō	old, oat, toe, low
ā	ape, pain, day, break		ô	coffee, all, taught, law, fought
ä	father, car, heart		ôr	order, fork, horse, story, pour
âr	care, pair, bear, their, where		oi	oil, toy
b	bat, above, job		ou	out, now
ch	chin, such, match		p	pail, repair, soap, happy
d	dear, soda, bad		r	ride, parent, more, marry
e	end, pet, said, heaven, friend		s	sit, pets, cent, pass
ē	equal, me, feet, team, piece, key		sh	shoe, fish, mission, nation
f	five, leaf, off, cough, elephant		t	tag, fat, button, dressed
g	game, ago, fog, egg		th	thin, panther, both
h	hat, ahead		<u>th</u>	this, mother, smooth
hw	white, whether, which		u	up, mud, love, double
i	it, big, English, him		ū	use, mule, cue, feud, few
ī	ice, fine, lie, my		ü	rule, true, food
îr	ear, deer, here, pierce		ù	put, would, should
j	joke, enjoy, gem, page, edge		ûr	burn, term, word, courage
k	kite, bakery, seek, tack, cat		v	very, favor, wave
l	lid, sailor, feel, ball, allow		w	wet, weather, reward
m	man, family, dream		y	yes, onion
n	not, final, pan, knife		z	zoo, jazz, rose, dogs, houses
ng	long, singer, pink		zh	vision, treasure, azure
o	odd, hot, watch		ə	about, taken, pencil, lemon, circus

©1998 McGraw-Hill School Division, a Division of the Educational and Professional Publishing Group of the McGraw-Hill Companies, Inc.

© McGraw-Hill School Division

My Word List

© McGraw-Hill School Division

© McGraw-Hill School Division